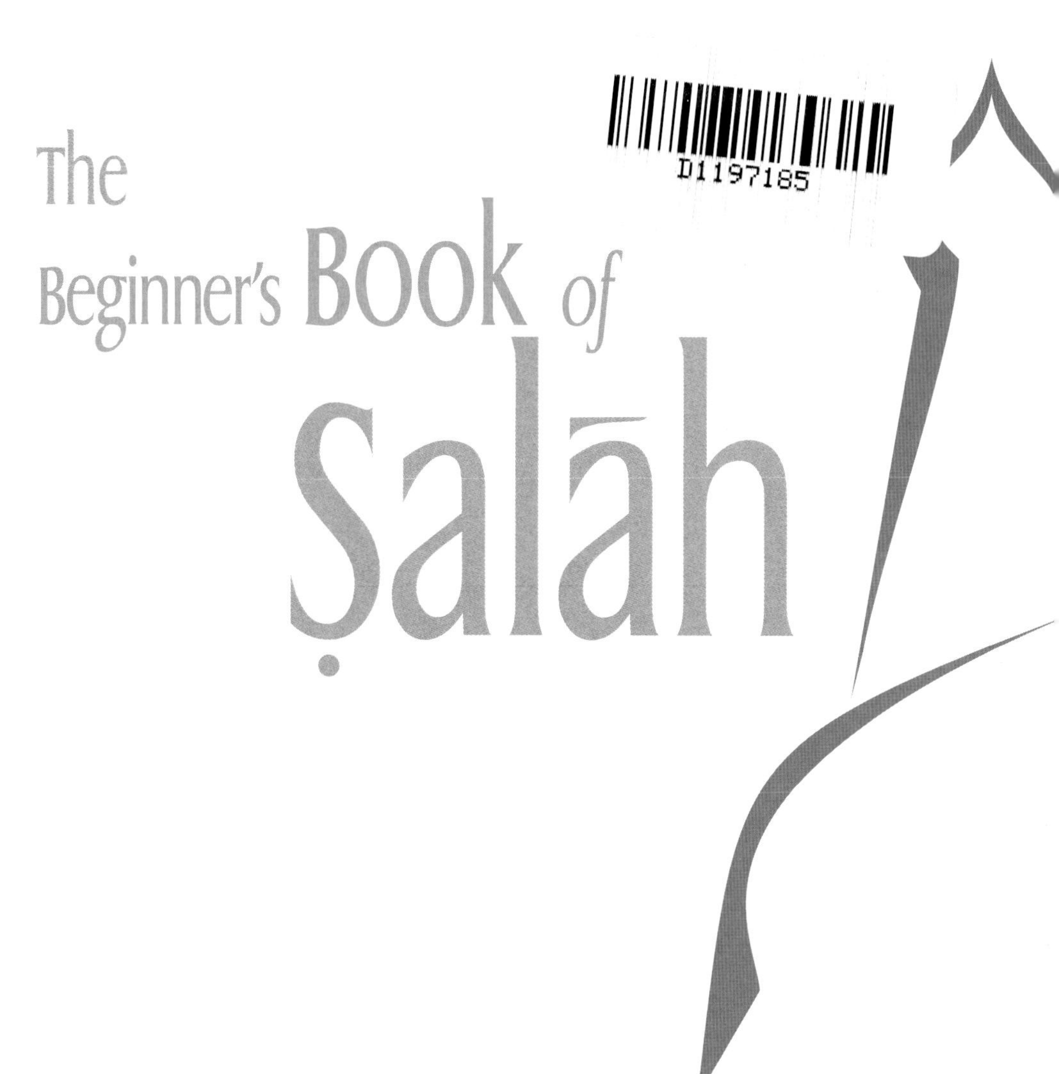

The Beginner's Book of Ṣalāh

Ghulam Sarwar

The Muslim Educational Trust

1st Edition London 1984 (10,000)

2nd Edition London 1987 (12,000)

3rd Edition London 1990 (12,000)
reprinted in London 1993 (15,000), 1996 (15,000)

4th Edition London 1998 (21,000)

5th Edition London 2000 (21,000)

The first five editions were published under the title 'The Children's Book of Ṣalāh'

6th Edition London 2003 (21,000)
6th Edition reprinted London 2005 (25,000)

Published by
The Muslim Educational Trust
130 Stroud Green Road
London N4 3RZ, UK
TEL: 020 7272 8502 FAX: 020 7281 3457
WEB: http://www.muslim-ed-trust.org.uk EMAIL: info@muslim-ed-trust.org.uk

British Library Cataloguing in Publication Data:
Sarwar, Ghulam
The Beginner's Book of Ṣalāh—6th Ed.
1. Prayer (Islām)—Juvenile literature
l. Title
297'.43 BP178

ISBN 0 907261 39 6

Printed and bound in Great Britain by
Midland Regional Printers
Jubilee House, Nottingham Road
Basford
Nottingham
NG7 7BT

Contents

بســـــمِ ٱللهِ ٱلرَّحمٰنِ ٱلرَّحِيمِ

Preface to the First Edition (Abridged)

The dissemination of the universal message of Islām in the West is integrally linked with the Islāmic orientation of English-speaking young Muslims. It is by no means an easy task. It is a daunting challenge which the Muslim Educational Trust has been trying its best to meet, with modest success. We bow down our heads to Allāh in praise. The credit for the achievements of His slaves rightly and justly belong to Him.

Ṣalāh is the second of the five fundamental duties of Islām. It is the foundation of *'Ibādah*, which includes all human activities performed to gain Allāh's pleasure. Prophet Muḥammad ﷺ said, "*Ṣalāh* is the key to Paradise." Indeed, in the constant and conscious performance of this obligatory duty lies the success of the believers. Allāh, our Merciful and Loving Creator, says: *"Successful are the believers who are humble in their prayers."* (*Sūratul Mu'minūn* 23:1–2)

I have been thinking for some time to write a book on *Ṣalāh* for English-speaking young Muslims in easy language in order to acquaint them with the basic details of how to perform it. The result is *The Children's Book of Ṣalāh.* I am humbled by the mercy of Almighty Allāh who enabled me to materialise my thinking. My success is for the readers to judge. Responsibility for all errors is unquestionably mine. I would gratefully appreciate any comments.

I have arranged the topics to learn in a systematic way, beginning with the meaning and importance of *Ṣalāh*. I have added at the end a chapter on *Ma'rūf* (Right) and *Munkar* (Wrong). I hope regular performance of *Ṣalāh* will inspire young Muslims to work for the establishment of *Ma'rūf* in society and the removal of *Munkar.*

I urge parents and teachers to take special care in teaching the correct pronunciation of various Islāmic terms and names used in the performance of *Ṣalāh*. I believe, given the will, it is not difficult.

I must point out here that the theoretical teaching of *Ṣalāh* by parents and teachers can be effective only if they practice it themselves. Many of us these days moan about children who are drifting away from the teachings of Islām. Rather than complaining we should set up examples for our children since *examples are better than precepts;* in the case of *Ṣalāh* there cannot be any better statement than this.

May Allāh accept my humble efforts and make it a source of my salvation in the life after death. *Wa mā tawfīqī illā billāh*—And my success in my task can only come from Allāh (*Sūrah Hūd* 11:88).

London
Jumādal Ākhirah 1404 AH
March 1984 CE

Ghulam Sarwar

بسم الله الرحمن الرحيم

Preface to the Sixth Edition (Reprinted)

No amount of praise and thanks I give to my Creator and Sustainer Allāh *subḥānahu wa ta'alā* will match His mercy and blessings on me. I implore Him to forgive, bless and protect me. I come from Him and to Him I must return to account for all my deeds on the day of reckoning. May the peace and blessings of Allāh be upon Muḥammad ﷺ, the final messenger of Allāh on earth.

Through *Shahādah* (the declaration of faith) we voluntarily and consciously enter into a binding contract with our Creator to submit ourselves loyally to His will and obey His commands in all areas of our life on this earth. *Ṣalāh*, the second of the five basic duties in Islām, provides us with the means to manifest this commitment and to prove what we testified in *Shahādah*.

Ṣalāh gives us the opportunity to show that we love our Creator who gave us everything we need without any imploration. We should always remain conscious of His power and do our best to obey His commands. It also helps us to taste the sweetness of our faith and feel the inexpressible feeling of peace, tranquillity, happiness and joy in our heart and gain Allāh's pleasure—the ultimate aim of every Muslim.

Muslims who perform their *Ṣalāh* correctly could change the present-day problem-full world where peace and happiness of heart and mind are almost non-existent because of the sheer dominance of materialism.

I beseech Allāh, my Most Merciful and Most Kind Creator, to enable young Muslims and those new Muslims whom He has blessed to come into the fold of Islām to enjoy His heavenly bliss by doing their *Ṣalāh* correctly with full consciousness of submission, obedience and humility.

The book is based on *Ḥanafī fiqh*, as the majority of Muslim children in the UK come from families who follow this school of thought. However, not only are there children from other backgrounds, most children will grow up communities where they can see some differences in some aspects of *Ṣalāh*, reflecting the richness and diversity of the Muslim community in the UK. I therefore make occasional mention in the text of some of these variations.

I have changed the title of my book from *The Children's Book of Ṣalāh* to *The Beginner's Book of Ṣalāh* to reflect its wider readership. The contents remain the same, with some small improvements to the text and the layout.

I am indebted to my colleague Usamah K. Ward for typesetting the book on computer and suggesting improvements. I am grateful to Syed Dohan Nuh for designing the cover.

May Allāh accept this revised and retitled version of *The Beginner's Book of Ṣalāh*, and may He make it a source of my *Najāh* (salvation) in the *Ākhirah* (life after death).

London
Ramadan 1426 AH
October 2005 CE

Ghulam Sarwar

Transliteration

Correct pronunciation of Arabic words is very important. Incorrect pronunciation changes the meaning of an Arabic word.

Transliteration marks are shown below as a guide to correct pronunciation. These marks help to show how the words should sound, but it is not possible to show on a printed page exactly how to pronounce words.

For example, the word *Allāh* should be pronounced correctly with the two *Ls* sounded distinctly, and the last *A* has to be a long sound. The name *Muḥammad* should be pronounced with a glottal sound of *H* rather than the normal *H* sound, with the two *Ms* sounded clearly.

I have used phonetic transliteration for the benefit of younger learners, e.g. *Sūratul Fātiḥah* rather than *Sūrah al-Fātiḥah*, *at-Tashahhud* rather than *al-Tashahhud*, etc.

Ideally, it is best to listen to an Arabic-speaking person, or someone who has learned how to say Arabic words correctly. Audio and video resources can be immensely helpful.

Arabic symbol	Transliteration symbol	English sound	Example	Arabic symbol	Transliteration symbol	English sound	Example
ا	a	add	*Akbar*	ف	f	far	*Fajr*
ب	b	bit	*Basmalah*	ق	q	–	*Qur'ān*
ت	t	tap	*Tarāwīḥ*	ك	k	king	*Ka'bah*
ث	th	think	*Thanā'*	ل	l	list	*Muslim*
ج	j	just	*Jumu'ah*	م	m	mist	*Masjid*
ح	ḥ	–	*Muḥammad*	ن	n	name	*Niyyah*
خ	kh	loch	*Khuṭbah*	و	w	wait	*Witr*
د	d	dawn	*Du'ā'*	ه ە	h	hinder	*Hidayah*
ذ	dh	worthy	*Dhikr*	ي	y	lawyer	*Tasmiyah*
ر	r	rip	*Rak'ah*	ة	t *if followed*, h *otherwise*		*Ṣalāh*
ز	z	zip	*Zakāh*	ء	'	–	*Qur'ān*
س	s	sat	*Sunnah*	َ *(fatḥa)*	a	tap	*Rajab*
ش	sh	shape	*Shahādah*	َا	ā	Saab	*Adhān*
ص	ṣ	–	*Ṣalāh*	ِ *(kasra)*	i	grin	*Jinn*
ض	ḍ	–	*Wuḍū'*	ِي	ī	deed	*Ḥadīth*
ط	ṭ	–	*Ṭahārah*	ُ *(ḍamma)*	u	pull	*Jumu'ah*
ظ	ẓ	–	*Ẓuhr*	ُو	ū	food	*Darūd*
ع	'	–	*'Aṣr*	َوْ	aw	how	*Ṣawm*
غ	gh	–	*Maghrib*	َيْ	ai	tie	*Shaiṭān*

Introduction to Ṣalāh 1

Islām is a complete way of life. It is the system of life Allāh has chosen for all mankind. The Qur'ān says: *"Surely, the way of life acceptable to Allāh is Islām."* (*Sūrah Āli 'Imrān* 3:19) Islām is the guidance *(Hidāyah)* for all affairs of life. It is based on five basic duties known as the pillars of Islām *(Arkānul Islām)*.

The first of these is *Shahādah*—the declaration of faith. It is at the heart of all Islāmic duties. *Shahādah* is testifying that *'there is no god but Allāh, Muḥammad is the messenger of Allāh'*. As soon as a person willingly testifies this, he becomes a Muslim.

He now has to do certain specific duties, one of which is *Ṣalāh*, known as the second pillar of Islām. Besides *Shahādah* and *Ṣalāh*, the other basic duties are *Zakāh* (Welfare Contribution), *Ṣawm* (Fasting in the month of *Ramaḍān*) and *Ḥajj* (Pilgrimage to Makkah).

Meaning and Importance of Ṣalāh

Ṣalāh (known also as *Namāz*, which is a Persian word) is the most important of all acts of worship *('Ibādah)*. *Ṣalāh* is prayer offered to Allāh using specific words and actions as shown by Prophet Muḥammad ﷺ.

It is very difficult to translate *Ṣalāh* into English. The nearest English words are 'prayer', 'blessings', 'supplication' or 'grace'. The word 'prayer' can mean any sort of prayer, but in Islām *Ṣalāh* refers to prescribed prayers which must be offered in a particular way at set times. It is better to use the Arabic word *Ṣalāh* at all times.

Ṣalāh is a practical sign of our faith *(Īmān)* in Allāh and Islām. It separates a believer *(Mu'min)* from the one who does not believe *(Kāfir)*. That is why Allāh commanded: *"Guard strictly your Ṣalāh, especially the middle Ṣalāh, and stand before Allāh with all devotion."* (*Sūratul Baqarah* 2:238)

Ṣalāh helps us to be good, modest, active, well behaved, disciplined and successful. Prophet Muḥammad ﷺ said, "The first thing that the slave of Allāh will be called upon to account for on the day of judgement will be *Ṣalāh*. If it was good, his actions will be taken as good; if it was bad, his actions will be taken as bad." *(at-Tirmidhī, Abū Dāwūd)* Allāh says in the Qur'ān: *"Surely, Ṣalāh keeps you away from indecency and evil."* (*Sūratul 'Ankabūt* 29:45)

You should start to say *Ṣalāh* when you are seven years old. You must be regular in saying your *Ṣalāh* when you are ten years old. A new Muslim should begin *Ṣalāh* after the declaration of *Shahādah*.

We should understand the importance of *Ṣalāh* and make a promise to offer it daily at fixed times. If we do so, Allāh will guide us in all matters and reward us with a pleasing reward which will make us really happy.

Purpose of Ṣalāh

It is important to make *Ṣalāh* a part of our life. The Qur'ān commands us to establish *Ṣalāh (Aqīmuṣ Ṣalāh)*. It means that Allāh commands us to perform *Ṣalāh* ourselves and ask others to do the same. We do not live alone; we belong to the society of mankind. *Ṣalāh* prepares society as well as each of us to obey the Laws of Allāh.

The purpose of establishing *Ṣalāh* is to remember Allāh *(Dhikrullāh)*. Allāh commands in the Qur'ān: *"Establish Ṣalāh to remember Me."* (*Sūrah Ṭā Hā* 20:14) To remember Allāh means to obey His commands in all affairs of life.

After testifying *Shahādah*, a person must be ready to say *Ṣalāh*. This is the first sign of the person's testimony. It means he is prepared to act on his testimony. This is why in Islām words and actions must go together. We must do what we say. Otherwise, our words are meaningless.

Ṣalāh must change our lifestyle. It must inspire us to obey Allāh in every way. If our *Ṣalāh* does not improve our behaviour, we must think carefully and find out where we are going wrong.

'Ibādah and Ṣalāh

'Ibādah, an Arabic word, means worship and obedience to Allāh. Allāh says in the Qur'ān: *"Indeed I created Jinn and human beings for no other purpose but to worship Me."* (*Sūratudh Dhāriyāt* 51:56). Anything we do is *'Ibādah*, if we do it for Allāh's sake. For example, obeying parents, respecting elders, eating *Ḥalāl* food, telling the truth and not telling lies, keeping promises, not being greedy, helping the poor and the needy, and honesty in business and politics are all acts of *'Ibādah*. Our purpose in life is to seek Allāh's pleasure through *'Ibādah*, and *Ṣalāh* prepares us to achieve this.

Four of the basic duties of Islām—*Ṣalāh, Zakāh, Ṣawm* and *Ḥajj*—are the main acts of *'Ibādah*. Doing these duties prepares us to obey Allah's commands in all affairs of our life. *Ṣalāh* is the most important of these four basic duties. It brings us closer to our Creator, and motivates us to obey Him. Allāh, our Creator, is happy and pleased when we obey His commands. He in return gives us peace and happiness in this life *(Dunyā)* and in the life hereafter *(Ākhirah)*.

Ṣalāh and Jihād

Jihād means doing one's best to see that *Ma'rūf* (Right) is established in a society and *Munkar* (Wrong) is removed from it. *'Ibādah* should prepare us for *Jihād* in the way of Allāh. Our *'Ibādah* is meaningful if it motivates us to work for the cause of Allāh. *Ṣalāh* is for *'Ibādah* and *'Ibādah* is for *Jihād fī sabī lillāh* (*Jihād* in the way of Allāh).

We have learned before that Islām is the complete way of life chosen by Allāh for mankind. In Islām, all parts of human life are connected to one another and are not separate. For example, the declaration of faith, *Shahādah*, is connected to each of the other basic duties: *Ṣalāh, Zakāh, Ṣawm* and *Ḥajj*. These duties make us ready for *Jihād fī sabī lillāh*.

Our life does not end with death. The real and unending life is the life after death. So, we must work towards the success in the never-ending life. There will be a test on the Day of Judgement when all our actions in this life will be judged by Allāh. Those of us who succeed will be rewarded by Paradise *(Jannah)*, a place of permanent happiness and joy, and those who fail will suffer torment in Hell *(Jahannam)*, a place of terrible suffering and pain. *Jihād fī sabī lillāh* is the way to bring about change in the society in which we live. It is the surest way to establish a just society to seek Allāh's pleasure and achieve success in the life after death.

Names and Timing of Ṣalāh

A Muslim must offer *Ṣalāh* five times a day at fixed times. Allāh says in the Qur'ān: *"Ṣalāh at set times has been made a duty on the believers."* (*Sūratun Nisā'* 4:103) These five daily *Ṣalāh* are:

1	**Fajr**	*between dawn and sunrise*	١ صَلَاةُ الْفَجْرِ
2	**Ẓuhr**	*between midday and mid-afternoon*	٢ صَلَاةُ الظُّهْرِ
3	**'Aṣr**	*between mid-afternoon and sunset*	٣ صَلَاةُ الْعَصْرِ
4	**Maghrib**	*just after sunset*	٤ صَلَاةُ الْمَغْرِب
5	**'Ishā'**	*between nightfall and dawn*	٥ صَلَاةُ الْعِشَاء

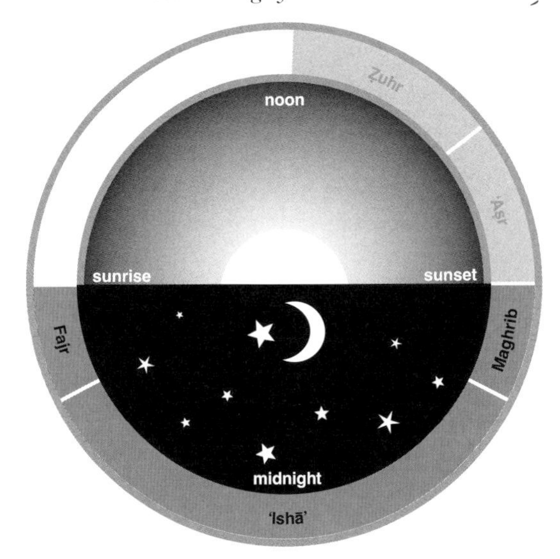

Preparation for Ṣalāh 2

Before we perform our *Ṣalāh*, there are some specific things we must do to follow exactly what Allāh has commanded and to follow how Prophet Muḥammad ﷺ himself did it.

Conditions for Ṣalāh (Farā'id)

1 Cleanliness of the whole body.
2 Cleanliness of clothes.
3 Cleanliness of the place of prayer.
4 For males, covering of the body from the navel to the knees. For females, covering the whole body except the face, feet below the ankles and the hands.
5 Facing the *Ka'bah (Qiblah).*
6 Making *Niyyah* (Intention).
7 Offering *Ṣalāh* at set times.
8 Saying *Ṣalāh* in Arabic.

Ṭahārah اَلطَّهَارَة

To say our *Ṣalāh* we must be pure and clean. The *Qur'ān* says: *"Indeed Allāh loves those who turn to Him in repentence and loves those who purify themselves."* (*Sūratul Baqarah* 2:222) Purification of the body and clothes is called *Ṭahārah*, and cleanliness is called *Naẓāfah*. They are not the same, but they are connected to one another.

Prophet Muḥammad ﷺ said that purification is the key to *Ṣalāh (Mishkāt al-Maṣābīḥ)*. He ﷺ also said that purification is one half of faith *(Muslim)*.

How can we have *Ṭahārah?* To have *Ṭahārah* for our body, we should do either:

Ghusl	full wash of the body with water; or,
Wuḍū'	ablution, which is washing parts of the body in a particular way.

Cleanliness of clothes also includes making sure that we do not have any traces of human or animal excrement (e.g. urine, stool) on our clothes. In Islām, physical cleanliness and cleanliness of the heart are equally important. Cleanliness of the heart means making sure that it is free from the idea of false gods; only the Creator, Allāh, should be firmly seated in our heart and we should only worship Him.

Ghusl اَلْغُسْل

There are certain circumstances when we must have *Ghusl* before saying *Ṣalāh*; under these circumstances *Wuḍū'* alone is not enough. These circumstances are:

1 After sexual intercourse between husband and wife.
2 After ejaculation of semen, for example 'wet dreams'.
3 For women, after menstruation and up to 40 days after childbirth.

There are other times when *Ghusl* is strongly recommended, such as before *Ṣalātul Jumu'ah* (Friday prayer), before *Ṣalātul 'Īd* (*'Īd* prayer), and before entering *Makkah*.

Ghusl involves washing the whole body. The three compulsory *(Farḍ)* aspects of *Ghusl* are:

1 rinsing the mouth thoroughly,
2 rinsing the nose up to the nasal bone,
3 washing all parts of the body (including the hair) thoroughly.

The steps to take for *Ghusl* are: make *Niyyah* (intention) that we are doing *Ghusl* to cleanse ourselves from impure or dirty things; wash our hands up to the wrists three times and then wash our private parts thoroughly; make *Wuḍū'* and, finally, pour water on all parts of the body, including our hair, and wash our whole body three times.

Muslims are not allowed to have a bath or a shower in the nude in the presence of others.

Wuḍū' اَلْوُضُوْء

Before we begin to say *Ṣalāh*, if we do not need to perform *Ghusl*, then we must at least make sure we have done *Wuḍū'*.

Allāh says in the *Qur'ān*: *"O you who believe, when you prepare for Ṣalāh, wash your faces and your hands to the elbows; wipe over your heads and wash your feet up to the ankles."* (*Sūratul Mā'idah* 5:6)

This verse tells us about the compulsory *(Farḍ)* parts of *Wuḍū'*. The additional actions performed by Prophet Muḥammad ﷺ are recommended *(Sunnah)*, and are mentioned in the books of *Aḥādīth*.

The four compulsory actions in *Wuḍū'* are:

1 wash our face
2 wash our arms from the hands up to the elbow
3 wipe our head
4 wash our feet up to the ankles.

Wuḍū' is essential for performing *Ṣalāh*. We must not say *Ṣalāh* without first making sure we have done our *Wuḍū'*. The steps to take are:

1 Make *Niyyah* (intention) saying the *Tasmiyah* (*Basmalah* or *Bismillāh*):

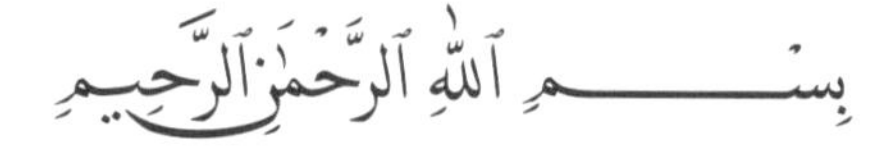

Bismillāhir raḥmānir raḥīm

In the name of Allāh, the Most Merciful, the Most Kind.

2 Then wash both hands up to the wrists three times making sure that water has reached between the fingers.

3 Put a handful of water into the mouth and rinse it thoroughly three times.

4 Sniff water into the nostrils three times to clean them and then wash the tip of the nose.

5 Wash the face three times from right ear to left ear and from forehead to throat.

6 Wash the right arm, and then left arm, thoroughly from hand to elbow three times.

7 Move the wet palms of both hands over the head, starting from the top of the forehead to the neck.

8 Rub the wet fingers into the grooves and holes of both ears and also pass the wet thumbs behind the ears.

9 Pass the backs of the wet hands over the nape.

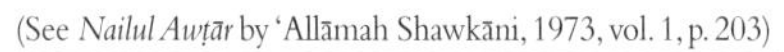
(See *Nailul Awṭār* by 'Allāmah Shawkāni, 1973, vol. 1, p. 203)

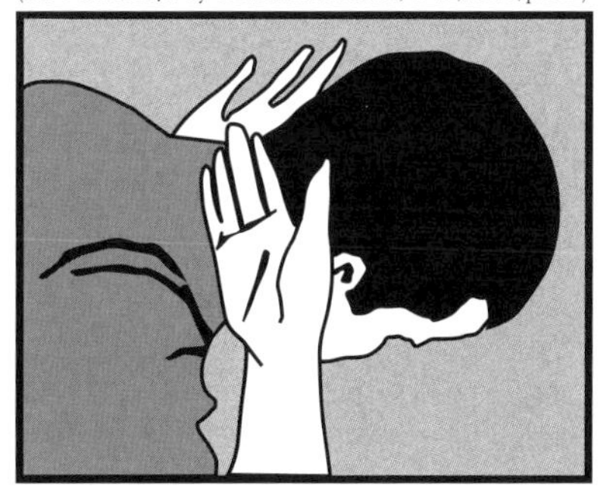

10 Wash both feet to the ankles starting from the right foot and making sure that water has reached between the toes and all other parts of the feet.

If we made a full *Wuḍū'* before putting on our socks, it is not necessary to take them off every time we repeat our *Wuḍū'*; it is enough to wipe the upper part of the socks with wet fingers. Leather socks are better for this, but any durable, untorn thick socks will also do. This type of wiping is valid for twenty-four hours only (three days in the case of a journey).

At the end of all the steps, recite:

أَشْهَدُ أَنْ لَآ إِلٰهَ إِلَّا اللهُ وَحْدَهُ لَا شَرِيْكَ لَهُ
وَأَشْهَدُ أَنَّ مُحَمَّدًا عَبْدُهُ وَرَسُوْلُهُ

Ash-hadu allā ilāha illallāhu waḥdahu lā sharīka lahu
wa ash-hadu anna Muḥammadan 'abduhu wa rasūluh.

I testify that there is no god but Allāh and He is One and has no partner and I testify that Muḥammad is His servant and messenger.

We should repeat our Wuḍū' after:

1 Natural discharges (e.g. urine, stool, wind and the like).
2 Flow of blood or pus from any part of the body.
3 Full mouth vomiting.
4 Falling asleep or losing consciousness.
5 Touching the sexual organs.

Even if we don't need to repeat our *Wuḍū'*, it is a Sunnah to do it before each *Ṣalāh*. Prophet Muḥammad ﷺ said: *"Indeed, on the Day of Resurrection, my followers will be called al-Ghurrul Muḥajjalūn from the traces of Wuḍū', so whoever can increase the area of his radiance should do so (i.e. by performing ablution regularly)." (al-Bukhārī)*

Tayammum (Dry Ablution) اَلتَّيَمُّم

We can perform our *Ṣalāh* with *Tayammum* (*Sūratun Nisā'* 4:43) when:

1 water is not available at all,
2 the water available is insufficient (e.g. available water is enough for drinking only), or
3 use of water is harmful (e.g. in sickness)

For *Tayammum* we are required to:

1 (a) Make *Niyyah* by saying: *Bismillāhir raḥmānir raḥīm*, then
(b) place both our hands lightly on earth, sand, stone or any other object having dust on it.
2 Blow the dust off our hands and wipe our face with the hands once the same way as we do in *Wuḍū'*.
3 Repeat 1(b) and wipe the right arm from wrist to elbow with the left hand and the left arm with the right hand.

Adhān (Call to Prayer) اَلْأَذَان

Prophet *Muḥammad* ﷺ, by his practice and sayings, showed that Muslim men and older boys should offer their compulsory *(Farḍ) Ṣalāh* in congregation in a mosque *(Masjid)*. Women and girls may offer their *Ṣalāh* in a mosque if they wish. All other *Ṣalāh* can be offered privately at home.

To call Muslims to *Ṣalāh*, Prophet *Muḥammad* ﷺ introduced the *Adhān* to signal that the time of *Ṣalāh* has arrived. The person who calls the *Adhān* is called the *Mu'adhdhin* (Caller). While doing so he faces the *Qiblah* (the direction towards the *Ka'bah* in *Makkah*). He raises his hands up to his ears and calls out:

اَللّٰهُ أَكْبَرُ   اَللّٰهُ أَكْبَرُ   اَللّٰهُ أَكْبَرُ   اَللّٰهُ أَكْبَرُ

Allāhu akbar   *Allāhu akbar*   *Allāhu akbar*   *Allāhu akbar*

Allāh is the Greatest Allāh is the Greatest Allāh is the Greatest Allāh is the Greatest

أَشْهَدُ اَنْ لَّآ إِلٰهَ إِلَّا اللّٰهُ   أَشْهَدُ اَنْ لَّآ إِلٰهَ إِلَّا اللّٰهُ

Ash-hadu allā ilāha illallāh   *Ash-hadu allā ilāha illallāh*

I testify that there is no god except Allāh   I testify that there is no god except Allāh

أَشْهَدُ اَنَّ مُحَمَّدًا رَسُوْلُ اللّٰهِ   أَشْهَدُ اَنَّ مُحَمَّدًا رَسُوْلُ اللّٰهِ

Ash-hadu anna Muḥammadar rasūlullāh   *Ash-hadu anna Muḥammadar rasūlullāh*

I testify that Muḥammad is Allāh's messenger   I testify that Muḥammad is Allāh's messenger

حَيَّ عَلَى الصَّلٰوةِ   حَيَّ عَلَى الصَّلٰوةِ

Ḥaiya 'alaṣ ṣalāh   *Ḥaiya 'alaṣ ṣalāh*

Rush to Ṣalāh   Rush to Ṣalāh

حَيَّ عَلَى الْفَلَاحِ   حَيَّ عَلَى الْفَلَاحِ

Ḥaiya 'alal falāḥ   *Ḥaiya 'alal falāḥ*

Rush to success   Rush to success

اَللّٰهُ أَكْبَرُ   اَللّٰهُ أَكْبَرُ

Allāhu akbar   *Allāhu akbar*

Allāh is the Greatest   Allāh is the Greatest

لَآ إِلٰهَ إِلَّا اللّٰهُ

Lā ilāha illallāh

There is no god except Allāh

During the *Adhān* for *Fajr Ṣalāh* the following words are added after *Ḥaiya 'alal falāḥ:*

اَلصَّلٰوةُ خَيْرٌ مِّنَ النَّوْمِ	اَلصَّلٰوةُ خَيْرٌ مِّنَ النَّوْمِ
Aṣ-ṣalātu khairum minan nawm	*Aṣ-ṣalātu khairum minan nawm*
Ṣalāh is better than sleep	Ṣalāh is better than sleep

Iqāmah اَلإِقَامَة

Iqāmah is the second call to *Ṣalāh* said inside the mosque at the beginning of *Ṣalāh* in congregation *(Jama'ah)*. When the *muṣallis* (persons saying *Ṣalāh*) stand in rows, the *Mu'adhdhin* says *Iqāmah* which is the same as the *Adhān* except that after *Ḥaiya 'alal falāḥ*, the following words are added:

قَدْ قَامَتِ الصَّلٰوة	قَدْ قَامَتِ الصَّلٰوة
Qad qāmatiṣ ṣalāh	*Qad qāmatiṣ ṣalāh*
Ṣalāh has begun	Ṣalāh has begun

Usually, the *Iqāmah* is said in a lower voice than the *Adhān*.

We should repeat the words the *Mu'adhdhin* calls out after him and when he says *Ḥaiya 'alaṣ ṣalāh* and *Ḥaiya 'alal falāḥ*, we should say:

لَا حَوْلَ وَلَا قُوَّةَ إِلَّا بِاللّٰهِ

Lā ḥawla wa lā quwwata illā billāh

There is no power and strength except Allāh

After hearing the *Mu'adhdhin* say *Aṣ-ṣalātu khairum minan nawm* we should say:

صَدَقْتَ وَبَرَرْتَ

Ṣadaqta wa bararta

You told the truth and you did good

When the *Mu'adhdhin* says *Qad qāmatiṣ ṣalāh* we should say:

أَقَامَهَا اللّٰهُ وَ أَدَامَهَا

Aqāmahallāhu wa adāmaha

May Allāh establish it and make it permanent

Du'ā' after Adhān الدُّعَآء بَعْدَ الأَذَان

اَللّٰهُمَّ رَبَّ هٰذِهِ الدَّعْوَةِ التَّآمَّةِ وَالصَّلَاةِ الْقَائِمَةِ آتِ مُحَمَّدَ
نِالْوَسِيْلَةَ وَالْفَضِيْلَةَ وَالدَّرَجَةَ الرَّفِيْعَةَ وَابْعَثْهُ مَقَامًا مَّحْمُوْدَ
نِالَّذِيْ وَعَدْتَّهُ وَارْزُقْنَا شَفَاعَتَهُ يَوْمَ الْقِيَامَةِ إِنَّكَ لَا تُخْلِفُ الْمِيْعَادَ .

Allāhumma
rabba hādhihid da'watit tāmmati
waṣ-ṣalātil qā'imah,
āti Muḥammada
nil wasīlata
wal faḍīlah,
wad-darajatar rafī'ah
wāb'athhu maqāmam maḥmūda nilladhī
wa 'attahu warzuqnā shafā'atahu
yawmal qiyāmah,
innaka lā tukhliful mī'ād.

O Allāh,
Lord of this complete call
and prayer of ours,
grant Muḥammad
the right of intercession,
and the most favoured position,
and raise him to the praiseworthy
place that You have promised him
and bestow upon us his intercession
on the Day of Resurrection,
for You do not fail in your promise.
(al-Bukhārī)

Details for Ṣalāh 3

Kinds of Ṣalāh

1 Farḍ (compulsory) اَلْفَرْض

These are the *Ṣalāh* which a Muslim must perform. There are two types of *Farḍ Ṣalāh:*

(i) *Farḍ 'Ain* فَرْضُ عَيْن These *Ṣalāh* must be performed by every Muslim, e.g. the five daily *Ṣalāh;*

(ii) *Farḍ Kifāyah* فَرْضُ كِفَايَة These *Ṣalāh* do not have to be performed by every Muslim; if some members of the community do them, others will be excused from doing them, e.g. *Ṣalātul Janāzah*.

2 Wājib* (obligatory) اَلْوَاجِب

These are *Ṣalāh* which also have to be performed and they come next in importance to *Farḍ*, e.g. *Ṣalātul 'Īd* and *Ṣalātul Witr*.

3 Sunnah (recommended) اَلسُّنَّة

These are *Ṣalāh* which Prophet *Muḥammad* ﷺ himself did or approved of. There are two types of *Sunnah Ṣalāh:*

(i) *Sunnah Mu'akkadah* سُنَّة مُؤَكَّدَة The *Ṣalāh* which the Prophet ﷺ regularly performed;

(ii) *Sunnah Ghair Mu'akkadah* سُنَّة غَيْر مُؤَكَّدَة The *Ṣalāh* which he ﷺ occasionally performed.

4 Nafl (optional) اَلنَّفْل

These are *Ṣalāh* which you can do on your own initiative to come closer to Allāh.

---

* The followers *Ḥanafī fiqh* make a distinction between *Farḍ* and *Wājib*. Followers of other *fiqh* do not make this distinction.

Essentials of Ṣalāh فَرَائِضُ الصَّلَاةِ

The following actions are *Farḍ* (compulsory) in *Ṣalāh:*

1 **Niyyah** اَلنِّيَّةُ
Having the correct intention for *Ṣalāh.*

2 **Takbīratul Iḥrām** تَكْبِيرَةُ الإِحْرَامِ
Saying *Allāhu akbar* at the beginning of the *Ṣalāh.*

3 **Qiyām** اَلْقِيَامُ
Standing upright.

4 **Qirā'ah** اَلْقِرَاءَةُ
Reciting *Sūratul Fātiḥah* and some verses from the *Qur'ān.*

5 **Rukū'** اَلرُّكُوعُ
Bowing so the back is horizontal, arms straight resting on the knees.

6 **Sujūd** اَلسُّجُوْدُ
Prostrating with the palms of both hands, the forehead, the tip of the nose, the knees and the toes of both feet touching the ground; there must be enough space between the arms and the chest and the legs and the belly so that they do not touch each other but remain apart.

7 **Qu'ūdul Akhīr** اَلْقُعُوْدُ الأَخِيرُ
Sitting in a kneeling position, the right foot upright on the toes and the left foot in a reclining position under the buttocks. This is done at the end of the last *rak'ah* of *Ṣalāh.*

8 **Salām** اَلسَّلَامُ
Turning the head to the right saying *Assalāmu 'alaikum wa raḥmatullāh* and then to the left repeating *Assalāmu 'alaikum wa raḥmatullāh.* This means the completion of *Ṣalāh.*

Wājibātus Ṣalāh وَاجِبَاتُ الصَّلَاةِ

The actions listed below should also be done in our *Ṣalāh.* They are called *Wājibātuṣ Ṣalāh* (necessary actions in *Ṣalāh*). They are next in importance to the eight *Farḍ* actions.

1 Reciting *Sūratul Fātiḥah* and some other verses from the *Qur'ān* in the first two *rak'ahs* of any *Farḍ Ṣalāh.*

2 Reciting *Sūratul Fātiḥah* in every *rak'ah* of every *Ṣalāh*.
3 Reciting a small *Sūrah*, a long verse or three short verses in each *rak'ah* of *Ṣalāh* except the third and fourth *rak'ah* of *Farḍ Ṣalāh*.
4 Reciting *Sūratul Fātiḥah* before the other *Sūrah* or verses of the *Qur'ān*.
5 Maintaining the order of *qiyām*, *qirā'h*, *rukū'*, *sujūd*, *qu'ūd* and *salām*.
6 Standing upright after *rukū'*.
7 Sitting up between two *sujūd*.
8 Performing each part of *Ṣalāh* calmly without haste*(I'tidāl)*.
9 Sitting whilst reciting the first *Tashahhud* in a three or four *rak'ah Ṣalāh*.
10 Reciting *Tashahhud* in both sittings in all the three and four *rak'ah Ṣalāh*.
11 Reciting *Sūratul Fātiḥah* and another *Sūrah* or verses loudly in the first two *Farḍ rak'ahs* of *Fajr*, *Maghrib*, and *'Ishā'*, in all the *rak'ahs* of *Jumu'ah*, *'Īd*, *Tarāwīḥ*, and in *Witr* during the Islāmic month of *Ramaḍān*.
12 To finish *Ṣalāh* by saying the words of *Salām*.
13 Reciting *Du'ā' al-Qunūt* in the third *rak'ah* of *Witr Ṣalāh*.
14 Saying six or twelve *Takbīr* in both *'Īd Ṣalāh*.
15 Doing *Sajdatus Sahw* in case of mistakes during *Ṣalāh*.

Sunan of Ṣalāh سُنَنُ الصَّلاَة

The following actions are the *Sunan* (plural of سُنَّة *Sunnah*) in *Ṣalāh:*

1 Raising both hands to the ears when saying *Allāhu akbar.*
2 Facing straight towards the *Qiblah* when saying *Allāhu akbar.*
3 The *Imām* (person who leads the prayer) saying aloud *Allāhu akbar* in different stages of *Ṣalāh*, *Sami' allāhu liman ḥamidah* (Allāh hears those who praise Him) whilst getting up from *rukū'*, and *Assalāmu 'alaikum wa raḥmatullāh* at the end.
4 Placing the right hand over the left hand, and below the navel or on the chest.
5 Reciting *Thanā' (Subḥānaka…)*, *Ta'awwudh (A'ūdhu billāhi…)* and *Tasmiyah (Bismillāh…)* silently.
6 Reciting only *Sūratul Fātiḥah* (silently) in the third and fourth *rak'ah* of all *Farḍ Ṣalāh*.
7 Saying *Āmīn* quietly or loudly on completing the recitation of *Sūratul Fātiḥah*.
8 Saying *Subḥāna rabbiyal 'aẓīm* three times in *rukū'* and *Subḥāna rabbiyal a'lā* three times in *Sujūd*.
9 Keeping the head and neck straight in *rukū'*.
10 The *Imām* saying *Sami' allāhu liman ḥamidah* and the followers *(Muqtadis)*

saying *Rabbanā lakal ḥamd* (O our Lord, praise be to You) whilst getting up from *rukū'*.

11 Whilst going into *Sujūd*, placing the knees on the floor first followed by the hands, nose and forehead.

12 Placing the palms near the knees when sitting between the *Sujūd*.

13 Sitting correctly in between two *Sujūd*, e.g. placing the feet correctly.

14 Lifting the forefinger of the right hand at the words *Ash-hadu allā ilāha illallāh* when reciting *Tashahhud*.

15 Reciting *aṣ-Ṣalāh 'alan Nabiyy (Darūd)* after the final *Tashahhud*.

16 Turning the head to the right and then to the left in the *Salām*.

Farḍ (Compulsory) Ṣalāh

A Muslim must pray five times a day. The compulsory prayers are called *Farḍ* in Arabic. Each unit of prayer is called a *rak'ah* (رَكْعَة). *Farḍ rak'ahs* are:

Fajr	....	**2** *rak'ahs*	
Ẓuhr	....	**4** *rak'ahs*	
'Aṣr	....	**4** *rak'ahs*	
Maghrib	....	**3** *rak'ahs*	
'Ishā'	....	**4** *rak'ahs*	
		17 *rak'ahs*	
Jumu'ah	....	**2** *rak'ahs*	(in place of *Ẓuhr* on Friday)

Sunnah Ṣalāh

Prophet *Muḥammad* ﷺ prayed extra *rak'ahs* in addition to *Farḍ* prayers. These prayers are called *Sunnah*. Prophet *Muḥammad* ﷺ always prayed two *rak'ahs* before the *Farḍ* of *Fajr* and three *rak'ahs* after the *Farḍ* of *'Ishā'* even on a journey. The three *rak'ahs* after *'Ishā'* are called *Witr* (odd number). Muslims also pray additional *rak'ahs* other than *Farḍ* and *Sunnah*. These are called *Nāfilah* (optional).

The Five Daily Ṣalāh

Fajr	Ẓuhr	‘Aṣr	Maghrib	‘Ishā’
2 Sunnah	4 Sunnah	4 Sunnah*		4 Sunnah*
2 Farḍ	**4 Farḍ**	**4 Farḍ**	**3 Farḍ**	**4 Farḍ**
	2 Sunnah		2 Sunnah	2 Sunnah
	2 Nafl		2 Nafl	2 Nafl
				3 Witr
				2 Nafl
4	12	8	7	17

(* these *Sunnah* before *‘Aṣr* and *‘Ishā’* are *Ghair Mu’akkadah*, not done regularly, only occasionally.)

In addition to the five daily *Ṣalāh*, there are *Ṣalāh* for other occasions, e.g. *Ṣalātul Jumu‘ah* every Friday (in place of *Ẓuhr*), *Ṣalātul ‘Īdul Fiṭr*, *Ṣalātul ‘Īdul Aḍḥā* and *Ṣalātut Tarāwīḥ* in the month of *Ramaḍān*. The number of *rak‘ahs* in these *Ṣalāh* are:

Jumu‘ah	‘Īdul Fiṭr	‘Īdul Aḍḥā	Tarāwīḥ
4 Sunnah			20 Sunnah
2 Farḍ	**2 Wājib**	**2 Wājib**	
4 Sunnah			
2 Sunnah			
2 Nafl			
14	2	2	20

Wājib is a term used in *Ḥanafī fiqh* for something compulsory to a degree less than *Farḍ*. Those who follow *Ḥanafī fiqh* consider *Ṣalātul Janāzah*, *Ṣalātul ‘Īdul Fiṭr*, *Ṣalātul ‘Īdul Aḍḥā* and *Witr Ṣalāh* as *Wājib*.

Tarāwīḥ is offered after the two *Sunnah rak‘ahs* of *‘Ishā’* but before the three of *Witr*.

Between *'Ishā'* and *Fajr*, a prayer called *Tahajjud* was regularly offered by the Prophet ﷺ. It was obligatory for the Prophet ﷺ. Devout Muslims try to follow the practice. Only those who wish to taste the sweetness of being closer to Allāh can appreciate the benefits of the *Tahajjud* prayer.

Times when you must not pray:

1 From the beginning of sunrise until 15–20 minutes after full sunrise.
2 When the sun is at its height (zenith or meridian).
3 From the beginning of sunset until it is fully set.
4 For women during menstruation, and for up to 40 days during post-childbirth bleeding.

Times when we should not say Nafl Ṣalāh

1 Between the *Farḍ* of *Ṣalātul Fajr* and sunrise.
2 Between the *Farḍ* of *Ṣalātul 'Aṣr* and sunset.
3 Before the *Farḍ* of *Ṣalātul Maghrib*.
4 During the *Khuṭbahs* of *Ṣalātul Jumu'ah* and *Ṣalātul 'Īd*.
5 Between *Ṣalātul Fajr* and *Ṣalātul 'Īd*.
6 After *Ṣalātul 'Īd* at the place where the *Ṣalāh* has been offered.
7 During the *Ḥajj* at Arafāt after *Ṣalātul Ẓuhr* and *Ṣalātul 'Aṣr* have been offered together.
8 Between *Ṣalātul Maghrib* and *Ṣalātul 'Ishā'* at *Muzdalifah* during *Ḥajj*.
9 When only a little time is left for saying the *Farḍ* of any *Ṣalāh*.

How to perform Ṣalāh 4

Now we should be ready to begin saying our *Ṣalāh*. We make sure we have *Wuḍū'*, a clean body, clean clothes and a clean place. This is how we should do our *Ṣalāh:*

1 Stand upright in a clean place (like a prayer mat) facing the direction of the *Ka'bah*. This is called *Qiyām* and the direction is called the *Qiblah* in Arabic. In the UK the *Qiblah* is towards the south-east. In other countries the direction will be different. We have to find out its direction before doing our *Ṣalāh*.

2 Say *Niyyah* (intention) either verbally or in the mind. *Niyyah* is said with the words:

				Fajr★	
	two★	*Farḍ*★		*Ẓuhr*	
"I intend to say	three	*Sunnah*	*rak'ahs* of *Ṣalātul*	*'Aṣr*	for Allāh facing the *Ka'bah*."
	four			*Maghrib*	
	(★say the one which is relevant)			*'Ishā'*	

3 Raise the hands up to the ears (women and girls up to the shoulders) and say:

اَللّٰهُ أَكْبَرُ

Allāhu Akbar

Allāh is the Greatest

This is called *Takbīratul Iḥrām*, meaning that all wordly things are now forbidden to us.

4 Place the right hand on the left hand just below the navel or on the chest (women and girls put their hands on their chest) and recite *Thanā':*

سُبْحَانَكَ اللّٰهُمَّ وَبِحَمْدِكَ وَتَبَارَكَ اسْمُكَ وَتَعَالٰى جَدُّكَ
وَلَآ إِلٰهَ غَيْرُكَ

Subḥānakallāhumma wa biḥamdika,	O Allāh, glory and praise are for You,
wa tabārakasmuka,	and blessed is Your name,
wa ta'ālā jadduka,	and exalted is Your Majesty;
wa lā ilāha ghairuk.	there is no god but You.
(or you may read *ghairuka)*	

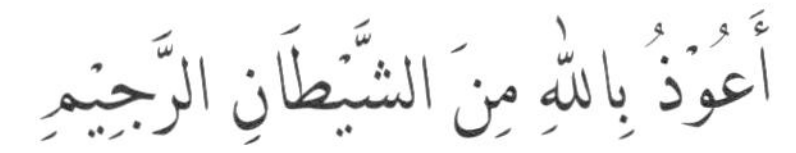

A'ūdhu billāhi minash shaiṭānir rajīm

I seek refuge in Allāh from the cursed Satan *(Shaiṭān).*

بِسْمِ ٱللَّهِ ٱلرَّحْمَٰنِ ٱلرَّحِيمِ

Bismillāhir raḥmānir raḥīm

In the name of Allāh, the Most Merciful, the Most Kind.

5 Recite the rest of *Sūratul Fātiḥah* (the opening chapter) of the *Qur'ān*:

ٱلْحَمْدُ لِلَّهِ رَبِّ ٱلْعَٰلَمِينَ .
ٱلرَّحْمَٰنِ ٱلرَّحِيمِ .
مَٰلِكِ يَوْمِ ٱلدِّينِ .
إِيَّاكَ نَعْبُدُ وَإِيَّاكَ نَسْتَعِينُ .
ٱهْدِنَا ٱلصِّرَٰطَ ٱلْمُسْتَقِيمَ .
صِرَٰطَ ٱلَّذِينَ أَنْعَمْتَ عَلَيْهِمْ
غَيْرِ ٱلْمَغْضُوبِ عَلَيْهِمْ وَلَا ٱلضَّآلِّينَ .

Alḥamdu lillāhi rabbil 'ālamīn.

Arraḥmānir raḥīm.
Māliki yawmid dīn.
Iyyāka na'budu wa iyyāka nasta'īn.

Ihdinaṣ ṣirāṭal mustaqīm.
Ṣirāṭal ladhīna an'amta 'alaihim,
ghairil maghḍūbi 'alaihim wa laḍ ḍāllīn.

All praise is for Allāh, the Lord of the Universe.
The Most Merciful, the Most Kind.
Master of the Day of Judgement.
You alone we worship, from You alone we seek help.
Guide us along the straight path.
The path of those whom You have favoured, not of those who earned Your anger nor of those who went astray (or who are misguided).

Then, quietly or loudly, we say:

آمين
Āmīn
Ameen

The recitation of *al-Fātiḥah* is a must in all prayers.

6 We recite any other *Sūrah* or some verses from the *Qur'ān*. For example:

Bismillāhir raḥmānir raḥīm
In the name of Allāh, the Most Merciful, the Most Kind.

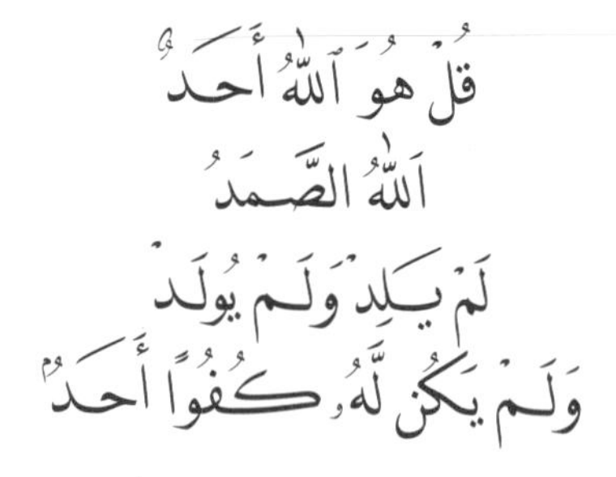

Qul huwallāhu aḥad.
Allāhuṣ ṣamad.
Lam yalid walam yūlad.
Walam yakul lahu kufuwān aḥad.

Say, He is Allāh, the One.
Allāh is Eternal and Absolute.
None is born of Him nor is He born.
And there is none like Him.
(Sūratul Ikhlāṣ 112*)*

7 We bow down saying *Allāhu Akbar,* then place our hands on our knees and say three times:

سُبْحَانَ رَبِّيَ الْعَظِيْمِ

Subḥāna rabbiyal 'aẓīm

Glory to my Lord, the Great

This position is called *Rukū'* (رُكُوْع).

8 We stand up from *Rukū'* saying:

سَمِعَ اللّٰهُ لِمَنْ حَمِدَهُ

Sami' allāhu liman ḥamidah

Allāh hears those who praise Him

followed by:

رَبَّنَا لَكَ الْحَمْدُ

Rabbanā lakal ḥamd

Our Lord, praise be to You

This is called *I'tidāl* as we return to the position of *Qiyām* (قِيَام) (standing).

9 We then prostrate saying *Allāhu akbar*, with our forehead, nose, palms of both hands, knees and toes touching the floor. We recite three times:

سُبْحَانَ رَبِّيَ الْأَعْلَى

Subḥāna rabbiyal a'lā

Glory to my Lord, the Highest

This position is called *Sujūd*. Our arms should not touch the floor.

10 We get up from the floor saying *Allāhu akbar* and sit upright with our knees bent and palms placed on them. After a moment's rest* we prostrate again saying *Allāhu akbar* and recite *Subḥāna rabbiyal a'lā* three times. We get up from this position saying *Allāhu akbar*.

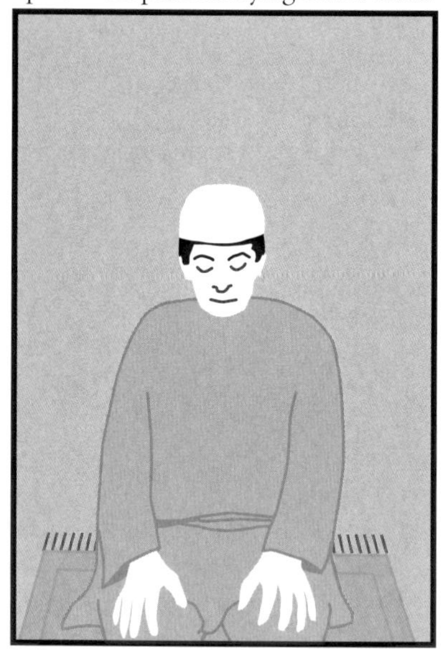

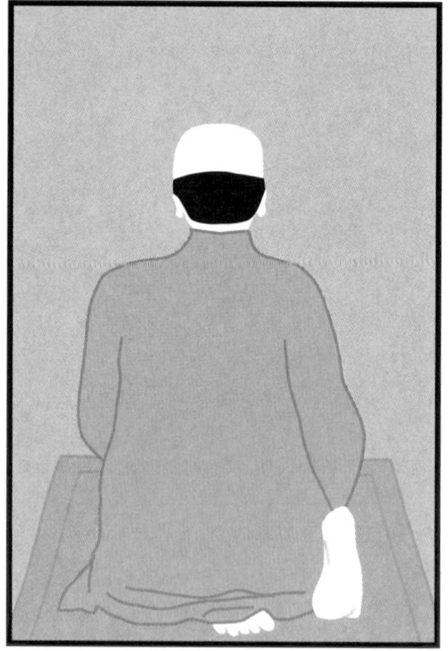

* Here we may say the *du'ā'*:

رَبِّ اغْفِرْ لِي وَارْحَمْنِي وَاهْدِنِي وَعَافِنِي وَارْزُقْنِي

Rabbighfir lī warḥamnī wahdinī wa'āfinī warzuqnī

My Lord forgive me, have mercy upon me, guide me, give me health and grant me sustenance.

This completes one *rak'ah* of *Ṣalāh*. The second *rak'ah* is performed in the same way, except we do not recite *Subḥānaka*, *Ta'awwudh* (*A'ūdhu billāhi…*) or *Tasmiyah* (*Bismillāh…*). After the second prostration we sit upright and recite quietly *at-Tashahhud*:

اَلتَّحِيَّاتُ لِلّٰهِ وَالصَّلَوٰتُ وَالطَّيِّبَاتُ. اَلسَّلَامُ عَلَيْكَ أَيُّهَا النَّبِيُّ
وَرَحْمَةُ اللّٰهِ وَبَرَكَاتُهُ. اَلسَّلَامُ عَلَيْنَا وَعَلٰى عِبَادِ اللّٰهِ الصَّالِحِيْنَ.
أَشْهَدُ أَنْ لَّآ إِلٰهَ إِلَّا اللّٰهُ وَأَشْهَدُ أَنَّ مُحَمَّدًا عَبْدُهُ وَرَسُوْلُهُ.

At-taḥiyyātu lillāhi	All compliments are for Allāh,
waṣ ṣalawātu waṭ ṭaiyibāt.	and prayers and goodness.
As-salāmu 'alaika aiyuhan nabiyyu	Peace be upon you, O Prophet,
wa raḥmatullāhi wa barakātuh.	and the Mercy of Allāh and His blessings.
As-salāmu 'alainā	Peace be upon us
wa 'alā 'ibādillāhiṣ ṣāliḥīn.	and on the righteous servants of Allāh.
Ash-hadu allā ilāha illallāhu	I testify that there is no god except Allāh
wa ash-hadu anna Muḥammadan	and I testify that Muḥammad
'abduhu wa rasūluh.	is His servant and messenger.
	(al-Bukhārī, Muslim)

If the *Ṣalāh* has three *rak'ahs* (*Maghrib*) or four *rak'ahs* (*Ẓuhr*, *'Aṣr* and *'Ishā'*), we stand up for the remaining *rak'ah* after *Tashahhud*. But for a two-*rak'ah Ṣalāh* we remain seated after the second *rak'ah* and recite *aṣ-Ṣalāh 'alan nabiyy* (blessings for the Prophet) or *Darūd* (a Persian word):

اَللّٰهُمَّ صَلِّ عَلٰى مُحَمَّدٍ وَّعَلٰى آلِ مُحَمَّدٍ كَمَا صَلَّيْتَ عَلٰى إِبْرَاهِيْمَ
وَعَلٰى آلِ إِبْرَاهِيْمَ إِنَّكَ حَمِيْدٌ مَّجِيْدٌ. اَللّٰهُمَّ بَارِكْ عَلٰى مُحَمَّدٍ وَّعَلٰى آلِ
مُحَمَّدٍ كَمَا بَارَكْتَ عَلٰى إِبْرَاهِيْمَ وَعَلٰى آلِ إِبْرَاهِيْمَ إِنَّكَ حَمِيْدٌ مَّجِيْدٌ.

	O Allāh,
Allāhumma	let Your blessings come on Muḥammad
ṣalli 'alā Muḥammadiw	and the family of Muḥammad
wa 'alā āli Muḥammadin,	as You blessed Ibrāhīm
kamā ṣallaita 'alā Ibrāhīma	and the family of Ibrāhīm.
wa 'alā āli Ibrāhīma,	Truly You are Praiseworthy and Glorious.
innaka ḥamīdum majīd,	O Allāh, bless Muḥammad
Allāhumma bārik 'alā Muḥammadiw	and the family of Muḥammad
wa 'alā āli Muḥammadin,	as You blessed Ibrāhīm
kamā bārakta 'alā Ibrāhīma	and the family of Ibrāhīm.
wa 'alā āli Ibrāhīma,	Truly You are Praiseworthy and Glorious.
innaka ḥamīdum majīd.	(*Muslim*)

After this we say any of the following *du'ā's* (supplications):

اَللّٰهُمَّ إِنِّي ظَلَمْتُ نَفْسِي ظُلْمًا كَثِيرًا وَلَا يَغْفِرُ الذُّنُوبَ إِلَّا أَنْتَ فَاغْفِرْ
لِي مَغْفِرَةً مِنْ عِنْدِكَ وَارْحَمْنِي إِنَّكَ أَنْتَ الْغَفُورُ الرَّحِيمُ.

Allāhumma innī ẓalamtu nafsī ẓulmān kathīrān
wa lā yaghfirudh dhunūba illā anta
faghfir lī maghfiratan min 'indika
warḥamnī
innaka antal ghafūrur raḥīm.

O Allāh, I have been very unjust to myself
and no one grants pardon for sins but You,
so forgive me with Your forgiveness
and have mercy on me.
Surely, You are the Forgiver, the Merciful.
(*al-Bukhārī, Muslim*)

رَبِّ ٱجْعَلْنِى مُقِيمَ ٱلصَّلَوٰةِ وَمِن ذُرِّيَّتِى رَبَّنَا وَتَقَبَّلْ دُعَآءِ.
رَبَّنَا ٱغْفِرْ لِى وَلِوَٰلِدَىَّ وَلِلْمُؤْمِنِينَ يَوْمَ يَقُومُ ٱلْحِسَابُ.

Rabbij'alnī muqīmaṣ ṣalāti
wa min dhurriyyatī,
rabbanā wa taqabbal du'ā'.
Rabbanaghfir lī wa liwālidaiya
wa lilmu'minīna yawma yaqūmul ḥisāb.

My Lord, make me steadfast in Ṣalāh
and also my descendents;
our Lord, and accept my prayer.
Our Lord, forgive me and my parents
and the believers on the Day of Judgement.
(*Sūrah Ibrāhīm* 14:40–41)

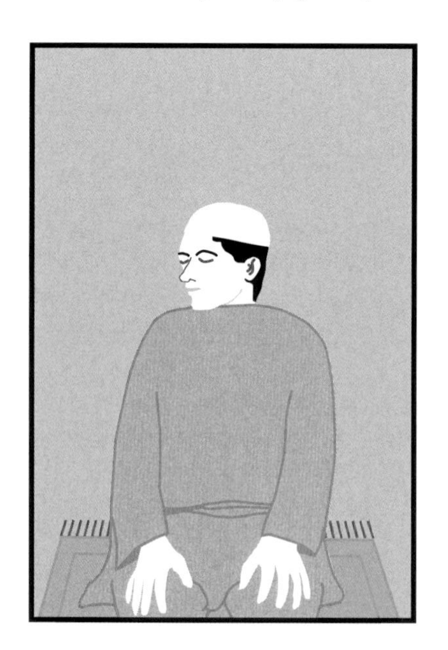

11 Now we turn your face to the right saying:

اَلسَّلَامُ عَلَيْكُمْ وَرَحْمَةُ اللّٰهِ

Assalāmu ʻalaikum wa raḥmatullāh

peace and the mercy of Allāh be upon you

and then to the left repeating the words.

This completes the two-*rak'ah Ṣalāh*. In the four-*rak'ah Ṣalāh* of *Ẓuhr*, *'Aṣr* and *'Ishā'*, the whole procedure is repeated except that when we get up to complete the remaining two *rak'ahs* (one *rak'ah* in *Maghrib* and *Witr*) after *Tashahhud*, we only recite *al-Fātiḥah* in *Farḍ* prayers and no other *Sūrah*. In a four-*rak'ah Sunnah Ṣalāh* we should recite another *Sūrah* or some verses of the *Qur'ān* after *al-Fātiḥah*.

In the first two *rak'ahs* of the *Farḍ* prayer of *Fajr*, *Maghrib* and *'Ishā'* the *Qur'ān* is recited aloud while in *Ẓuhr* and *'Aṣr* it is recited silently. In all prayers, *Tasbīḥ (Subḥāna rabbiyal 'aẓīm* and *Subḥāna rabbiyal a'lā)*, *Tashahhud* and *Darūd* are said quietly. When the *Fajr*, *Maghrib* and *'Ishā'* prayers are said in congregation, only the *Imām* (one who leads the prayer) recites the *Qur'ān* aloud. This also applies to *Jumu'ah* اَلْجُمُعَة prayer (Friday prayer in place of *Ẓuhr*).

Some duʻā' after Ṣalāh بَعْضُ الْأَدْعِيَة بَعْدَ الصَّلَاة

It is good practice to ask for forgiveness and mercy from Allāh at the end of the *Ṣalāh*. We can make *du'ā'* in our own words and in our own language but it is better for us to memorise some *du'ā's* in Arabic.

رَبَّنَآ ءَاتِنَا فِي ٱلدُّنْيَا
حَسَنَةً وَفِي ٱلْأَخِرَةِ حَسَنَةً
وَقِنَا عَذَابَ ٱلنَّارِ.

Rabbanā ātinā fiddunyā ḥasanah,
wa fil ākhirati ḥasanah,
wa qinā 'adhābannār.

Our Lord, grant us good in this world,
and good in the Hereafter,
and save us from the punishment of
Hellfire. (*Sūratul Baqarah* 2:201)

رَبَّنَا ظَلَمْنَآ أَنْفُسَنَا وَإِن لَّمْ تَغْفِرْ لَنَا وَتَرْحَمْنَا لَنَكُونَنَّ مِنَ الْخَاسِرِينَ .

Rabbanā ẓalamnā anfusanā
wa illam taghfirlanā
wa tarḥamnā
lanakūnanna minal khāsirīn.

Our Lord, we have wronged ourselves
and if You do not forgive us
and have no mercy upon us,
surely we will be among the losers.
(*Sūratul A'rāf* 7:23)

اَللّٰهُمَّ أَنْتَ السَّلَامُ وَمِنْكَ السَّلَامُ تَبَارَكْتَ يَا ذَا الْجَلَالِ وَالْإِكْرَامِ .

Allāhumma antas salāmu
wa minkas salāmu
tabārakta
yādhal jalāli wal ikrām.

O Allāh, You are the source of peace
and from You comes peace,
exalted You are,
O Lord of Majesty and Honour.
(Muslim)

لَآ إِلٰهَ إِلَّا اللّٰهُ وَحْدَهُ لَا شَرِيكَ لَهُ، لَهُ الْمُلْكُ وَلَهُ الْحَمْدُ وَهُوَ عَلَى كُلِّ شَيْءٍ قَدِيرٌ، اَللّٰهُمَّ لَا مَانِعَ لِمَا أَعْطَيْتَ، وَلَا مُعْطِيَ لِمَا مَنَعْتَ، وَلَا يَنْفَعُ ذَا الْجَدِّ مِنْكَ الْجَدُّ .

Lā ilāha illallāhu
waḥdahu lā sharīka lah,
lahul mulku wa lahul ḥamdu
wa huwa 'alā kulli shai'in qadīr.
Allāhumma lā māni'a
limā a'ṭait,
wa lā mu'ṭiya limā mana't,
wa lā yunfa'u dhal jaddi minkal jadd.

There is no god except Allāh
and He is One and has no partner,
sovereignty is His, all praise is His
and He has power over all things.
O Allāh, none can stop You giving
what You want to give,
nor give what You do not want given,
and none with means can do anything
with their means against You.
(*al-Bukhārī* and *Muslim*)

Ṣalātul Witr صَلَاةُ الْوِتْر

The *Witr* (odd number) prayer has three *rak'ahs*. The first two *rak'ahs* are like the first two *rak'ahs* of the *Maghrib* prayer. Then, after *Tashahhud* in the second *rak'ah*, we stand up saying *Allāhu akbar* for the third *rak'ah*. We recite *Sūratul Fātiḥah* and some other verses from the *Qur'ān* but before going to *Rukū'* we raise our hands up to the ears saying *Allāhu akbar* and recite the following *du'ā'* after placing our hands below the navel or on the chest. This *du'ā'* is called the *Qunūt*:

اَللّٰهُمَّ إِنَّا نَسْتَعِينُكَ وَنَسْتَغْفِرُكَ وَنُؤْمِنُ بِكَ وَنَتَوَكَّلُ عَلَيْكَ وَنُثْنِي
عَلَيْكَ الْخَيْرَ وَنَشْكُرُكَ وَلاَ نَكْفُرُكَ وَنَخْلَعُ وَنَتْرُكُ مَنْ يَّفْجُرُكَ .
اَللّٰهُمَّ إِيَّاكَ نَعْبُدُ وَلَكَ نُصَلِّي وَنَسْجُدُ وَإِلَيْكَ نَسْعٰى وَنَحْفِدُ وَنَرْجُوْ
رَحْمَتَكَ وَنَخْشٰى عَذَابَكَ إِنَّ عَذَابَكَ بِالْكُفَّارِ مُلْحِقٌ .

Allāhumma innā nasta'īnuka	O Allāh, we seek Your help
wa nastaghfiruka	and ask Your forgiveness
wa nu'minu bika wa natawakkalu 'alaika	and we believe in You and trust in You,
wa nuthnī 'alaikal khaira	and we praise You in the best way
wa nashkuruka wa lā nakfuruka	and we thank You and we are not ungrateful
wa nakhla'u wa natruku	and we cast off and forsake
man yafjuruk.	him who disobeys You.
Allāhumma iyyāka na'budu	O Allāh, You alone we worship
wa laka nuṣallī wa nasjudu	and to You we pray and we prostrate,
wa ilaika nas'ā wa naḥfidu	and to You we turn in haste,
wa narjū raḥmataka	and hope for Your mercy
wa nakhshā 'adhābaka;	and we fear Your punishment.
inna 'adhābaka bil kuffāri mulḥiq.	Your punishment overtakes the unbelievers.
	(al-Baihaqī)

Then we say *Allāhu akbar* and bow down in *Rukū'* and complete the rest of the prayer like the *Maghrib* prayer. The above *du'ā'* is used by Muslims who follow *Ḥanafī fiqh*. Another *du'ā'* used by some Muslims is:

اَللّٰهُمَّ اهْدِنِي فِيمَنْ هَدَيْتَ، وَعَافِنِي فِيمَنْ عَافَيْتَ وَتَوَلَّنِي فِيمَنْ
تَوَلَّيْتَ، وَبَارِكْ لِي فِيمَا أَعْطَيْتَ، وَقِنِي شَرَّ مَا قَضَيْتَ، فَإِنَّكَ تَقْضِي
وَلاَ يُقْضٰى عَلَيْكَ، إِنَّهُ لاَ يَذِلُّ مَنْ وَالَيْتَ، تَبَارَكْتَ رَبَّنَا وَتَعَالَيْتَ .

Allāhummahdinī fīman hadait,	O Allāh, guide me with those You have guided,
wa 'āfinī fīman 'āfait,	pardon me with those You have pardoned,
wa tawallanī fīman tawallait,	be an ally to me with those whom You are an ally to,
wa bārik lī fīmā a'ṭait,	bless me for what You have bestowed,
wa qinī sharra mā qaḍait,	and protect me from the evil You have decreed,

fa'innaka taqḍī wa lā yuqḍā 'alaik,	for verily You decree and none can decree over You,
innahu lā yadhillu man wālait,	indeed to he whom You show allegiance is never abased,
tabārakta rabbanā wa ta'ālait.	O Our Lord blessed and Exalted are You.
	(Abū Dāwūd, at-Tirmidhī, Ibn Mājah)

Sajdatus Sahw (prostration of forgetfulness) سَجْدَةُ السَّهْو

Since we are human beings, we are not above mistakes and errors. If we forget to do something in our *Ṣalāh*, we can make up for it by making two extra *sujūd* (prostrations) as we do in any *rak'ah* of *Ṣalāh*. This is called *Sajdatus Sahw*. This is done at the end of the last *rak'ah* of *Ṣalāh*. What we have to do is:

1. We say *Tashahhud* (but not *Darūd*), then turn our face to the right and say *Assalāmu 'alaikum wa raḥmatullāh*;
2. We turn our face to the front, make two extra *sujūd* (with *Tasbīḥ—Subḥāna rabbiyal a'lā*);
3. Then we recite *Tashahhud* again with *Darūd* and *du'ā'*;
4. Then we turn our face, first to the right and then to the left, saying *Assalāmu 'alaikum wa raḥmatullāh.*

A slightly different sequence is followed by some Muslims: at the end of the last *rak'ah* we say *Tashahhud* and *Darūd*. Then we turn our face to the right and say *Assalāmu 'alaikum wa raḥmatullāh*. Then we face to the front, make two extra *sujūd* (with *Tasbīḥ – Subḥāna rabbiyal a'lā*). Finally, we turn our face, first to the right and then to the left, saying *Assalāmu 'alaikum wa raḥmatullāh*.

Sajdatus Sahw is necessary if we forget to do any essentials of *Ṣalāh*, for example, the recitation of parts of the *Qur'ān* after *al-Fātiḥah*, forgetting to say the first *Tashahhud* in a four-*rak'ah Ṣalāh*, or saying *salām* after two *rak'ahs* in a four-*rak'ah Ṣalāh*.

Our *Ṣalāh* will not be valid if we do any of the following:

1. Miss out *Niyyah* (intention).
2. Miss out *Takbīratul Iḥrām*.
3. Forget to recite *al-Fātiḥah*.
4. Forget or do not make *rukū'* or *sujūd*.
5. Do not face the *Qiblah*.
6. Do not have *Wuḍū'*.
7. Talk during *Ṣalāh*.
8. Eat or drink during *Ṣalāh*.
9. Do not sit for *Tashahhud*.

In these circumstances, we must repeat our *Ṣalāh*. *Sajdatus Sahw* is not enough.

Qaḍā' (قَضَاء): making up for missed Ṣalāh

We must always try to offer *Ṣalāh* at the right time and make every effort not to miss our *Ṣalāh*. If we miss our *Ṣalāh*, we must do it at the first opportunity. Performing a missed *Ṣalāh* after its proper time is called *Qaḍā'*. We must make up our *Farḍ Ṣalāh*.

Ṣalāh in congregation

When we perform *Ṣalāh* in congregation, there are certain matters we should bear in mind.

We must pray in straight rows behind the *Imām*. We should not leave any gaps—we fill any space in a row before starting a new row.

We always follow the *Imām*. We do not perform any action before him.

We should be considerate to those around us. Wearing perfume to smell nice is recommended. We avoid eating foods that leave a strong smell when going to congregational *Ṣalāh*, such as raw onions or garlic.

What should we do if you arrive after the Ṣalāh has started?

We should always try to be on time for *Ṣalāh*. We should be ready when the *Iqāmah* is called. But sometimes we might arrive after the *Ṣalāh* has started.

a We join the *Ṣalāh* straight away by saying *Takbīratul Iḥrām*. Then we move to the position the congregation has reached. So, if they are bowing in *rukū'*, we move to *rukū'*; if they are prostrating in *sujūd*, we move to *sujūd*.

b We follow the *Imām* until the end. If we missed any *rak'ahs*, we need to do them. A *rak'ah* is missed if we join it after *rukū'* (after the *Imām* says *Sami' allāhu liman ḥamidah*). If we catch a *rak'ah* before that, then we do not have to do that *rak'ah* again.

c If we have missed any *rak'ahs*, when the *Imām* says *Salām* at the end of the last *rak'ah* we don't say *Salām*. Instead, we stand up and do the *rak'ahs* we missed*, with *Tashahhud* if it's more than two *rak'ahs*.

d When we have completed our missed *rak'ahs*, we remain sitting. We say *Tashahhud* and *Darūd*. Then we finish with *Salām*.

Example

We join the *'Asr Ṣalāh* whilst the congregation is in the third *rak'ah* in *sujūd*. Standing, we say *Takbīratul Iḥrām (Allāhu akbar)*, then we go straight to *sujūd*. We follow the *Imām* until the he says *Salām*.

As the *Imām* says the second *Salām*, we stand to complete our *Ṣalāh*. We missed three *rak'ahs* (we joined the third *rak'ah* after *rukū'*, which means we missed that *rak'ah*).

We pray the first and second *rak'ah* exactly as we would for any *Farḍ Ṣalāh**. Whilst sitting, we recite *Tashahhud*. Then we stand and do one more *rak'ah*, just like the third *rak'ah* of any *Farḍ Ṣalāh*. Finally, we say *Tashahhud* and *Darūd*, then finish with *Salām*. This completes our *Ṣalāh*.

---

* Some schools of *Fiqh* pray the missed *rak'ahs* in a different order

Ṣalāh on Special Occasions 5

Ṣalātul Jumu'ah (Friday Prayer) صَلَاةُ الْجُمُعَةِ

Ṣalātul Jumu'ah or Friday Prayer (not *Jumma* or *Juma*, as some Muslims incorrectly say) is offered in congregation. All adult Muslim men must take part. It is offered on Friday during *Ẓuhr* time. It is not a must for women, but they can join this prayer if it does not upset their household duties.

People assemble for this *Ṣalāh* immediately after noon. Upon arrival at the mosque or the prayer hall, they offer four or more *rak'ahs Sunnah* prayer and then the *Imām* (prayer leader) delivers a *Khuṭbah* (sermon). After the *Khuṭbah*, the *Imām* leads two *rak'ahs Farḍ* prayer. After the *Farḍ* prayer, six or more *rak'ahs* of *Sunnah* and *Nafl* prayers are offered individually by each person.

Muslims are a community. *Ṣalātul Jumu'ah* is a community prayer. Every week, on Friday, Muslims living in an area get together to offer this prayer. This day is likened to a weekly *'Īd* (festival) for Muslims.

Mosques were the centre of all Islāmic activity during our Prophet's ﷺ time, but this is not so nowadays.

Friday prayer is an occasion for the assembly of Muslims in any given area. It gives them an opportunity to meet, discuss and solve their community problems. It develops unity, cooperation and understanding.

In an Islāmic state, the Head of State or his representative or the local leader is supposed to lead the five daily prayers and the Friday prayer at the central mosque of the capital city or the central mosque of the locality. Prophet *Muḥammad* ﷺ, the first head of the Islāmic state in *Madīnah*, used to lead all the prayers in *al-Masjidun Nabawī*.

How nice it would be to live in a country where the Head of State, his representative or the local leader leads the prayer in the central mosque of the capital city or of the area! May Allāh help us to revive this practice in all Muslim countries. *Āmīn!*

Ṣalātut Tahajjud صَلَاةُ التَّهَجُّدِ

This is a special *Ṣalāh* which Prophet *Muḥammad* ﷺ was told by Allāh to do to attain a position of praise and glory, and to be able to carry out the difficult task of prophethood. Allāh says in the *Qur'ān*: *"And in some parts of the night (also) offer the prayer with (recitation of the Qur'ān) as an additional prayer for you (O Muḥammad). It may be that your Lord will raise you to a position of praise and glory."* (*Sūratul Isrā'* 17:19) Allāh told the Prophet ﷺ to do *Qiyāmul Lail*, which means standing in the night in prayer, for about half of the night, reciting the *Qur'ān* in a slow, pleasant tone (*Sūratul Muzzammil* 73:1-6). Allāh says that the really good Muslims often do *Qiyāmul Lail*, asking for Allāh's favour and forgiveness, and hoping to gain His pleasure (*Sūratudh Dhāriyāt* 51:15–16; *Sūratul Furqān* 25:64; *Sūratus Sajdah* 32:16; *Sūratuz Zumar* 39:9).

This *Ṣalāh* has special importance in helping us to achieve righteousness *(Birr)* and piety *(Taqwā)*, so that we will match our actions with our words, trying our best to come closer to our Loving and Kind Creator Who has given us all that we have.

Ṣalātut Tahajjud is offered between *Ṣalātul Ishā'* and *Ṣalātul Fajr*. It is done two *rak'ahs* at a time. The *Qur'ān* should be recited calmly in a slow, measured manner, and usually we should try to recite as much as we can. If we are sure we will not miss it, we may delay *Ṣalātul Witr* until straight after *Ṣalātul Tahajjud*, so long as we do it before dawn.

Ṣalātut Tahajjud helps us to forget the distractions of our temporary life on this earth so we can prepare ourselves for eternal bliss in the never-ending life in the *Ākhirah* (life after death). In this prayer in the quietness of the night, an obedient and devoted slave of Allāh can ask his beloved Maker for everything he needs to carry out his duties as the *Khalīfah* (agent) of Allāh on this earth. This is the prayer where we can sob and shed tears, which Allāh loves, asking for His forgiveness and mercy, and hoping to be granted a position of peace, happiness and bliss in this life and in the *Ākhirah*. May Almighty Allāh help us to do this difficult but important and beneficial *Ṣalāh* as often as we can. *Āmīn*.

Ṣalātul Janāzah (Funeral Prayer) صَلَاةُ الْجَنَازَة

We have already briefly mentioned death and *Ṣalātul Janāzah*. We all shall die. When a Muslim dies, the body is given a simple ritual wash and then a funeral prayer called *Ṣalātul Janāzah* is offered in congregation. This *Ṣalāh*, unlike other *Ṣalāh*, has neither any *rukū'* (bowing) nor any *sujūd* (prostration) and you don't have to recite *Tashahhud*.

It is a collective duty *(Farḍu Kifāyah)* on all the Muslims of the locality of the dead person. If a number of them join in, the duty is discharged on behalf of all. If no one joins in everyone of the locality will be considered sinful before Allāh. This is how the prayer is offered:

1 We make *Niyyah* (intention) that we are saying this prayer to Allāh for the dead person.

2 We Stand in rows facing the *Qiblah*. The coffin is placed in front of the congregation on a bier.

3 We say *Allāhu akbar* after the *Imām* (this is *Takbīratul Iḥrām*; there are three more *takbīrāt* after this), raising our hands up to our ears. Then we lower them, placing them on or below our chest, putting the right hand on the left, and recite the following:

سُبْحَانَكَ اَللّٰهُمَّ وَبِحَمْدِكَ وَتَبَارَكَ اسْمُكَ وَتَعَالٰى جَدُّكَ وَجَلَّ ثَنَآءُكَ وَلَآ إِلٰهَ غَيْرُكَ .

Subḥānakallāhumma wa biḥamdika	O Allāh, glory and praise are for You,
wa tabārakasmuka	and blessed is Your Name,
wa ta'ālā jadduka	and exalted is Your Majesty,
wa jalla thanā'uka	and Glorious is Your Praise
wa lā ilāha ghairuk	and there is no god but You.
(or you may read *ghairuka).*	

(Some Muslims recite Ṣūratul Fātiḥah instead of this.)

4 Now the *Imām* will say *Allāhu akbar* loudly; we follow him repeating the words quietly. There is no need to raise our hands up to our ears this time. Then, we recite *Darūd*.

5 After this, the third *takbīr* will be said loudly by the *Imām* and those in the congregation will repeat it quietly. Then, if the dead person is an adult male Muslim, we recite the following *du'ā'*:

اَللّٰهُمَّ اغْفِرْ لِحَيِّنَا وَمَيِّتِنَا وَشَاهِدِنَا وَغَآئِبِنَا وَصَغِيْرِنَا وَكَبِيْرِنَا وَذَكَرِنَا وَأُنْثَانَا . اَللّٰهُمَّ مَنْ أَحْيَيْتَهُ مِنَّا فَأَحْيِهِ عَلَى الْإِسْلَامِ وَمَنْ تَوَفَّيْتَهُ مِنَّا فَتَوَفَّهُ عَلَى الْإِيْمَانِ .

Allāhummaghfir liḥaiyinā	O Allāh, forgive those of us who are alive
wa maiyitinā	and those who have passed away,
wa shāhidinā wa ghā'ibinā	those present and those absent,
wa ṣaghīrinā wa kabīrinā	and our young and elderly,
wa dhakarinā wa unthāna.	the males and the females.
Allāhumma	O Allāh,
man aḥyaitahu minnā	he whom You keep alive from among us,
fa'aḥyihi 'alal islāmi	make him live according to Islām,
wa man tawaffaitahu minnā	and he whom You wish to die from among us,
fatawaffahu 'alal īmān.	let him die in the state of *Īmān* (faith).
	(at-Tirmidhī, Abū Dāwūd)

If the dead person is an adult female Muslim, then the second part of this *du'ā'* is replaced by:

اَللّٰهُمَّ مَنْ أَحْيَيْتَهَا مِنَّا فَأَحْيِهَا عَلَى الْإِسْلَامِ وَمَنْ تَوَفَّيْتَهَا مِنَّا فَتَوَفَّهَا عَلَى الْإِيْمَانِ.

Allāhumma	O Allāh,
man aḥyaitahā minnā	she whom You keep alive from among us,
fa'aḥyihā 'alal islāmi,	make her live according to Islām,
wa man tawaffaitahā minnā	and she whom You wish to die from among us,
fatawaffahā 'alal īmān.	let her die in the state of *īmān*.

If the deceased is a boy, then we recite the following:

اَللّٰهُمَّ اجْعَلْهُ لَنَا فَرَطًا وَّاجْعَلْهُ لَنَآ أَجْرًا وَّذُخْرًا وَّاجْعَلْهُ لَنَا شَافِعًا وَّمُشَفَّعًا.

Allāhummaj'alhu lanā faraṭan	O Allāh, make him our forerunner
waj'alhu lanā ajran wa dhukhran	and make him for us a reward and a treasure
waj'alhu lanā shāfi'an	and make him one who will plead for us
wa mushaffa'ā.	and accept his pleading.

If the deceased is a girl, then we recite the following:

اَللّٰهُمَّ اجْعَلْهَا لَنَا فَرَطًا وَّاجْعَلْهَا لَنَآ أَجْرًا وَّذُخْرًا وَّاجْعَلْهَا لَنَا شَافِعَةً وَّمُشَفَّعَةً.

Allāhummaj'alhā lanā faraṭan	O Allāh, make her our forerunner
waj'alhā lanā ajran wa dhukhran	and make her for us a reward and a treasure
waj'alhā lanā shāfi'atan	and make her one who will plead for us
wa mushaffa'ah.	and accept her pleading.

6 After reciting whichever *du'ā'* is appropriate for the dead person, the *Imām* says the fourth *takbīr* loudly and those in the congregation repeat it quietly.

7 Then the *Imām* turns his face first to the right saying *Assalāmu 'alaikum wa raḥmatullāh*, and then to the left repeating the same words. We follow the *Imām*, repeating the words quietly.

This completes *Ṣalātul Janāzah*.

Ṣalātut Tarāwīḥ صَلَاةُ التَّرَاوِيْح

Tarāwīḥ is a special prayer, usually of twenty *rak'ahs*, offered in the Islāmic month of *Ramaḍān* after the two *Sunnah rak'ahs* of *'Ishā'* but before the three of *Witr*. It is usually done in *Jama'ah* (congregation) in a mosque led by an *Imām* who is often a *Ḥāfiẓ* (a person who has memorised the whole of the *Qur'ān*). *Tarāwīḥ* is done two *rak'ahs* at a time, like the two *rak'ahs* of *Ṣalātul Fajr*, with a very short rest after each four *rak'ahs*. The *Imām* recites the *Qur'ān* aloud and the *Muqtadīs* (followers) listen to the recitation and follow him as in any *Farḍ Ṣalāh*. Some Muslims pray eight, ten, twelve up to a maximum of thirty-six *rak'ahs* of this *Sunnah Ṣalāh* (for more details, see *Fiqhus Sunnah* by as-Sayyid Sābiq, English translation, American Trust Publications, 1989, Vol II, pages 27–29).

Ṣalātut Tarāwīḥ is a part of the rigorous training programme during the fasting month of *Ramaḍān*. It helps Muslims to strengthen their faith and control their worldly desires, in order to do *Jihād fī sabī lillāh* (striving one's utmost in the way of Allāh).

Ṣalātul 'Īdain ('Īd prayers) صَلَاةُ الْعِيْدَيْن

There are two main festivals of Islām in each year: *'Īdul Fiṭr* and *'Īdul Aḍḥā*. On both occasions a two-*rak'ah Ṣalāh* is offered in congregation, after sunrise but before noon. No *Adhān* or *Iqāmah* is said. The special point to note is that *Ṣalātul 'Īd* is said with six or twelve *takbīr (Allāhu akbar)*. You say three or seven *takbīr* in the first *rak'ah* after *Thanā' (Subḥānaka)* or *Takbīratul Iḥrām*, and three or five *takbīr* in the second *rak'ah* before you do *rukū'*. The rest is exactly like the two *Farḍ* of *Ṣalātul Jumu'ah* except that the *Khutbah* (Sermon) is given after the prayer. You may recall in *Ṣalātul Jumu'ah* the *Khutbah* is given before the two *Farḍ rak'ahs*. All Muslims, including women and children, should join *Ṣalātul 'Īd* to give thanks to Allāh for giving them an opportunity to be happy and cheerful on these days, and to share the joy with those who are needy and less fortunate.

Ṣalātul Musāfir صَلَاةُ الْمُسَافِر

A Muslim who is on a journey is allowed to shorten a four-*rak'ah Farḍ Ṣalāh* to two *rak'ahs*. Two- and three-*rak'ah Farḍ Ṣalāh* remain as they are. This means that the four-*rak'ah Farḍ* of *Ẓuhr*, *'Aṣr* and *'Ishā'* will be shortened to two *rak'ahs* each. The *Farḍ* of *Fajr* and *Farḍ* of *Maghrib* remain unchanged. Allāh says in the *Qur'ān*: *"And when you go forth in the land, it is no sin for you to shorten your Ṣalāh."* (*Sūratun Nisā'* 4:101)

Prophet *Muḥammad* ﷺ used to say two *rak'ahs* of *Sunnah* before the two *rak'ahs* of *Farḍ* at the time of *Fajr*, and three *rak'ahs* of *Witr* even when on a journey.

We can shorten *Farḍ Ṣalāh* on a journey if:

i we are forty-eight miles or more away from home;

ii we have the intention of staying less than fifteen days in one place during the journey. If after fifteen days, we change our intention and stay a few days more, we can still shorten the four *rak'ah Farḍ* of *Ẓuhr*, *'Aṣr* and *'Ishā'* and leave out all *Sunnah* and *Nafl Ṣalāh*.

If a *Musāfir* (traveller) prays behind an *Imām* who is a *Muqīm* (local resident) for *Ẓuhr*, *'Aṣr* or *'Ishā' Ṣalāh*, the *Musāfir* says all four *rak'ahs*. However, if the *Imām* is a *Musāfir*, then a *Muqtadī* (follower) who is a *Musāfir* also shortens the *Ṣalāh* like the *Imām*, but a *Muqtadī* who is a *Muqīm* must complete the four *rak'ahs* by standing up when the *Imām* says *Assalāmu 'alaikum*..., and doing the last two *rak'ahs* just like the normal *Farḍ Ṣalāh* only reciting *Sūratul Fātiḥah*.

Ṣalātul Istikhārah صَلَاةُ الْإِسْتِخَارَة

This *Ṣalāh* is offered to seek Allāh's guidance in any matter where we cannot be sure which is the best course of action to take. Only Allāh knows the consequences of our actions, and which choices are best for us both in this life and in the *Ākhirah*.

We first perform two *rak'ahs* of *Sunnah* or *Nafl Ṣalāh*, with the intention of making *Istikhārah*, then we say a special *du'ā'*. Prophet *Muḥammad* ﷺ used to instruct his companions to pray for guidance *(Istikhārah)* in all their concerns just as he would teach them a *Sūrah* from the *Qur'ān*. He ﷺ said:

> "If any of you intends to undertake a matter, then let him pray two *rak'ahs* other than the *Farḍ* (i.e. *Sunnah* or *Nafl*), after which he should say:
>
> اَللّٰهُمَّ إِنِّيْ أَسْتَخِيْرُكَ بِعِلْمِكَ وَأَسْتَقْدِرُكَ بِقُدْرَتِكَ، وَأَسْأَلُكَ مِنْ
> فَضْلِكَ الْعَظِيْمِ، فَإِنَّكَ تَقْدِرُ وَلَآ أَقْدِرُ وَتَعْلَمُ وَلَآ أَعْلَمُ وَأَنْتَ
> عَلَّامُ الْغُيُوْبِ. اَللّٰهُمَّ إِنْ كُنْتَ تَعْلَمُ أَنَّ هٰذَا الْأَمْرَ (ويسمّى
> حاجته) خَيْرٌ لِّيْ فِيْ دِيْنِيْ وَمَعَاشِيْ وَعَاقِبَةِ أَمْرِيْ فَاقْدُرْهُ لِيْ
> وَيَسِّرْهُ لِيْ ثُمَّ بَارِكْ لِيْ فِيْهِ، وَإِنْ كُنْتَ تَعْلَمُ أَنَّ هٰذَا الْأَمْرَ شَرٌّ لِّيْ
> فِيْ دِيْنِيْ وَمَعَاشِيْ وَعَاقِبَةِ أَمْرِيْ فَاصْرِفْهُ عَنِّيْ وَاصْرِفْنِيْ عَنْهُ
> وَاقْدُرْ لِيَ الْخَيْرَ حَيْثُ كَانَ ثُمَّ أَرْضِنِيْ بِهِ."

Allāhumma	O Allāh,
innī astakhīruka	indeed I seek Your guidance
bi 'ilmika	through Your knowledge,
wa astaqdiruka biqudratika,	and ability through Your power,
wa as'aluka min faḍlikal 'aẓīm,	and beg of Your infinite bounty;
fa innaka taqdiru wa lā aqdiru	for You have power and I have none,
wa ta'lamu wa lā a'lamu	You know and I know not,
wa anta 'allāmul ghuyūb.	and You are the Knower of hidden things.
Allāhumma	O Allāh,
in kunta ta'lamu anna hādhal amra	if in Your knowledge this matter
(mention your matter here)	*(mention your matter here)*
khairul lī fī dīnī wa ma'āshī	is good for my faith and my livelihood
wa 'āqibati amrī	and for the outcome of my affairs,
faqdurhu lī	then decide it for me
wa yassirhu lī	and make it easy for me
thumma bārik lī fīhi,	and bless me therein;
wa in kunta ta'lamu anna hādhal amra	but if in Your knowledge this matter
sharrul lī fī dīnī wa ma'āshī	is bad for my faith and my livelihood
wa 'āqibati amrī	and for the outcome of my affairs,
faṣrifhu 'annī	then turn it away from me,
waṣrifnī 'anhu	and turn me away from it,
waqdur liyal khaira	and decide for me the good
ḥaithu kāna	wherever it may be,
thumma arḍinī bih.	and cause me to be pleased with it.
	(al-Bukhārī, Muslim)

Once you have made *Istikhārah*, Allāh may cause you to keep firm to your choice or to change your mind. After you have gone through with whatever decision you finally made, you should trust that Allāh led you to what is best, and should have no regret. *"Then, when you have taken a decision, put your trust in Allāh. Certainly, Allāh loves those who put their trust (in Him)."* (*Sūrah Āli 'Imrān* 3:159)

Lessons of Ṣalāh فَضَائِلُ الصَّلَاةِ

Ṣalāh is the most important of the five basic duties of Islām after *Shahādah*. We come closer to Allāh by performing it regularly, correctly and with full awareness of its significance and meaning. At this stage, let us refresh our memory about the purpose of our creation and the need for performing Islāmic duties. Allāh has created us to worship Him. He says in the *Qur'ān: "Indeed I created Jinn and human beings for no other purpose but to worship Me."* (*Sūratudh Dhāriyāt* 51:56) So, whatever duty we carry out, we must bear in mind that we are doing it for the sake of Allāh. Only then can we expect to gain the desired benefits of the performance of *Ṣalāh*.

Allāh says in the *Qur'ān: "Successful indeed are the believers who are humble in prayers."* (*Sūratul Mu'minūn* 23:1–2)

Prophet *Muḥammad* ﷺ said, "The five set prayers may be compared to a stream of fresh water flowing in front of your house, into which you plunge five times each day. Do you think that you would leave any dirt on your body?" When his companions replied, "None at all!" the Prophet ﷺ said, "Indeed the five prayers remove sins, just as water removes dirt." *(Muslim)*

The lessons of *Ṣalāh* are:

1 It brings men and women closer to Allāh.
2 It keeps human beings away from indecent, shameful and forbidden activities.
3 It is a training programme designed to control evil desires and passions.
4 It purifies the heart, develops the mind and comforts the soul.
5 It is a constant reminder of Allāh and His greatness.
6 It develops discipline and willpower.
7 It is a guide to the most upright way of life.
8 It is a proof of true equality, solid unity and universal brotherhood.
9 It is the source of patience, courage, hope and confidence.
10 It is a means of cleanliness, purity and punctuality.
11 It develops gratitude, humility and refinement.
12 It is the demonstration of our obedience to our Creator.
13 It teaches us to match our actions with our words.
14 It is the solid programme of preparing oneself for *Jihād*—striving one's utmost to please Allāh.

If our *Ṣalāh* does not improve our conduct we must think seriously about where we are going wrong.

Eleven Sūrahs of the Qur'ān 6

إِحْدَى عَشَرَ سُورَةً مِنَ ٱلْقُرْآنِ

(سُورَةُ الْفَاتِحَة وَمِنْ سُورَةُ النَّاس إِلَى سُورَةُ الْفِيل)

1 Sūratul Fātiḥah (1) سُورَةُ الْفَاتِحَة

بِسْمِ ٱللَّهِ ٱلرَّحْمَٰنِ ٱلرَّحِيمِ
ٱلْحَمْدُ لِلَّهِ رَبِّ ٱلْعَٰلَمِينَ
ٱلرَّحْمَٰنِ ٱلرَّحِيمِ
مَٰلِكِ يَوْمِ ٱلدِّينِ
إِيَّاكَ نَعْبُدُ وَإِيَّاكَ نَسْتَعِينُ
ٱهْدِنَا ٱلصِّرَٰطَ ٱلْمُسْتَقِيمَ
صِرَٰطَ ٱلَّذِينَ أَنْعَمْتَ عَلَيْهِمْ غَيْرِ ٱلْمَغْضُوبِ عَلَيْهِمْ وَلَا ٱلضَّآلِّينَ

Bismillāhir raḥmānir raḥīm.
Alḥamdu lillāhi rabbil ʻālamīn.
Arraḥmānir raḥīm.
Māliki yawmid dīn.
Iyyāka naʻbudu wa iyyāka nastaʻīn.
Ihdinaṣ ṣirāṭal mustaqīm.
Ṣirāṭal ladhīna anʻamta ʻalaihim, ghairil maghḍūbi ʻalaihim wa laḍ ḍāllīn.

In the name of Allāh, the Most Merciful, the Most Kind.
All praise is for Allāh, the Lord of the Universe.
The Most Merciful, the Most Kind.
Master of the Day of Judgement.
You alone we worship, from You alone we seek help.
Guide us along the straight path.
The path of those whom You have favoured, not of those who earned Your anger nor of those who went astray (or who are misguided).

2 Sūratun Nās (114) سُورَةُ النَّاس

بِسْمِ ٱللَّهِ ٱلرَّحْمَٰنِ ٱلرَّحِيمِ

قُلْ أَعُوذُ بِرَبِّ ٱلنَّاسِ. مَلِكِ ٱلنَّاسِ. إِلَٰهِ ٱلنَّاسِ. مِن شَرِّ ٱلْوَسْوَاسِ ٱلْخَنَّاسِ. ٱلَّذِي يُوَسْوِسُ فِي صُدُورِ ٱلنَّاسِ. مِنَ ٱلْجِنَّةِ وَالنَّاسِ.

Bismillāhir raḥmānir raḥīm.
Qul a'ūdhu birabbin nās,
Malikin nās,
Ilāhin nās,
Min sharril waswāsil khannās,
Alladhī yuwaswisu fī ṣudūrin nās,
Minal jinnati wan nās.

In the name of Allāh, the Most Merciful, the Most Kind.
Say, I seek refuge in the Lord of mankind,
the King of mankind,
the God of mankind,
from the mischief of the sneaking whisperer (who whispers secretly),
who whispers into the hearts of mankind,
from among Jinn and mankind.

3 Sūratul Falaq (113) سُورَةُ الفَلَق

بِسْمِ ٱللَّهِ ٱلرَّحْمَٰنِ ٱلرَّحِيمِ

قُلْ أَعُوذُ بِرَبِّ الْفَلَقِ. مِن شَرِّ مَا خَلَقَ. وَمِن شَرِّ غَاسِقٍ إِذَا وَقَبَ. وَمِن شَرِّ النَّفَّاثَاتِ فِي الْعُقَدِ. وَمِن شَرِّ حَاسِدٍ إِذَا حَسَدَ.

Bismillāhir raḥmānir raḥīm.
Qul a'ūdhu birabbil falaq,
Min sharri mā khalaq,
Wa min sharri ghāsiqin idhā waqab,
Wa min sharrin naffāthāti fil 'uqad,
Wa min sharri ḥāsidin idhā ḥasad.

In the name of Allāh, the Most Merciful, the Most Kind.
Say, I seek refuge in the Lord of the Daybreak,
from the evil of what He has created,
and from the evil of the darkness when it is intense,
and from the evil of those who blow on knots (practise witchcraft),
and from the evil of the envier when he envies.

4 Sūratul Ikhlāṣ (112) سُورَةُ الإِخْلَاص

بِسْمِ ٱللَّهِ ٱلرَّحْمَٰنِ ٱلرَّحِيمِ

قُلْ هُوَ ٱللَّهُ أَحَدٌ . ٱللَّهُ ٱلصَّمَدُ . لَمْ يَلِدْ وَلَمْ يُولَدْ . وَلَمْ يَكُن لَّهُۥ كُفُوًا أَحَدٌۢ .

Bismillāhir raḥmānir raḥīm.
Qul huwallāhu aḥad.
Allāhuṣ ṣamad.
Lam yalid wa lam yūlad.
Wa lam yakul lahū kufuwan aḥad.

In the name of Allāh, the Most Merciful, the Most Kind.
Say, He is Allāh, the One.
Allāh is Eternal and Absolute (lives forever and is above all needs).
None is born of Him nor is He born.
And there is none like Him.

5 Sūratul Lahab (111) سُورَةُ اللَّهَب / سُورَةُ الْمَسَد

بِسْمِ ٱللَّهِ ٱلرَّحْمَٰنِ ٱلرَّحِيمِ

تَبَّتْ يَدَآ أَبِي لَهَبٍ وَتَبَّ . مَآ أَغْنَىٰ عَنْهُ مَالُهُۥ وَمَا كَسَبَ . سَيَصْلَىٰ نَارًا ذَاتَ لَهَبٍ . وَٱمْرَأَتُهُۥ حَمَّالَةَ ٱلْحَطَبِ . فِي جِيدِهَا حَبْلٌ مِّن مَّسَدٍۭ .

Bismillāhir raḥmānir raḥīm.
Tabbat yadā abī lahabin watabb.
Mā aghnā 'anhu māluhū wa mā kasab.
Sayaṣlā nāran dhāta lahab,
Wamra'atuhū ḥammālatal ḥaṭab,
Fī jīdihā ḥablum mim masad.

In the name of Allāh, the Most Merciful, the Most Kind.
May the hands of Abū Lahab perish—doomed he is.
His wealth and his gains shall not help him.
He shall enter a blazing fire,
and his wife, the carrier of firewood,
shall have a rope of palm fibre around her neck.

6 Sūratun Naṣr (110) سُورَةُ النَّصر

بِسْمِ ٱللَّهِ ٱلرَّحْمَٰنِ ٱلرَّحِيمِ

إِذَا جَآءَ نَصْرُ ٱللَّهِ وَٱلْفَتْحُ . وَرَأَيْتَ ٱلنَّاسَ يَدْخُلُونَ فِي دِينِ ٱللَّهِ أَفْوَاجًا . فَسَبِّحْ بِحَمْدِ رَبِّكَ وَٱسْتَغْفِرْهُ إِنَّهُۥ كَانَ تَوَّابًۢا .

Bismillāhir raḥmānir raḥīm.
Idhā jā'a naṣrullāhi wal fatḥ.
Wa ra'aitan nāsa yadkhulūna fī dīnillāhi afwājā.
Fasabbiḥ biḥamdi rabbika wastaghfirh,
Innahū kāna tauwābā.

In the name of Allāh, the Most Merciful, the Most Kind.
When the help of Allāh comes and the conquest,
and you see the people accepting the religion of Allāh in large numbers,
then glorify the praises of your Lord, and seek His forgiveness.
He is ever ready to forgive.

7 Sūratul Kāfirūn (109) سُورَةُ الْكَافِرُوْن

بِسْمِ ٱللَّهِ ٱلرَّحْمَٰنِ ٱلرَّحِيمِ

قُلْ يَـٰٓأَيُّهَا ٱلْكَـٰفِرُونَ . لَآ أَعْبُدُ مَا تَعْبُدُونَ .
وَلَآ أَنتُمْ عَـٰبِدُونَ مَآ أَعْبُدُ . وَلَآ أَنَا۠ عَابِدٌ مَّا عَبَدتُّمْ .
وَلَآ أَنتُمْ عَـٰبِدُونَ مَآ أَعْبُدُ . لَكُمْ دِينُكُمْ وَلِىَ دِينِ .

Bismillāhir raḥmānir raḥīm.
Qul yā'aiyuhal kāfirūn,
Lā a'budu mā ta'budūn, wa lā antum 'ābidūna mā a'bud,
Wa lā ana 'ābidum mā 'abattum, wa lā antum 'ābidūna mā a'bud,
Lakum dīnukum wa liya dīn.

In the name of Allāh, the Most Merciful, the Most Kind.
Say: O unbelievers!
I do not worship what you worship,
and you do not worship what I worship.
Nor will I worship what you worship,
and you will not worship what I worship.
You have your own religion and I have mine.

8 Sūratul Kawthar (108) سُوْرَةُ الْكَوْثَر

بِسْمِ ٱللهِ ٱلرَّحْمَٰنِ ٱلرَّحِيمِ

إِنَّآ أَعْطَيْنَٰكَ ٱلْكَوْثَرَ . فَصَلِّ لِرَبِّكَ وَٱنْحَرْ .

إِنَّ شَانِئَكَ هُوَ ٱلْأَبْتَرُ

Bismillāhir raḥmānir raḥīm.
Innā a'ṭaināka l kawthar.
Faṣalli lirabbika wanḥar.
Inna shāni'aka huwal abtar.

In the name of Allāh, the Most Merciful, the Most Kind.
Indeed we have given you the Kawthar (Fountain of Abundance).
So pray to your Lord and make sacrifice.
Surely your hater is the one cut off (i.e. without an heir).

9 Sūratul Mā'ūn (107) سُوْرَةُ الْمَاعُوْن

بِسْمِ ٱللهِ ٱلرَّحْمَٰنِ ٱلرَّحِيمِ

أَرَءَيْتَ ٱلَّذِي يُكَذِّبُ بِٱلدِّينِ . فَذَٰلِكَ ٱلَّذِى يَدُعُّ ٱلْيَتِيمَ .

وَلَا يَحُضُّ عَلَىٰ طَعَامِ ٱلْمِسْكِينِ . فَوَيْلٌ لِّلْمُصَلِّينَ .

ٱلَّذِينَ هُمْ عَن صَلَاتِهِمْ سَاهُونَ . ٱلَّذِينَ هُمْ يُرَآءُونَ . وَيَمْنَعُونَ ٱلْمَاعُونَ .

Bismillāhir raḥmānir raḥīm.
Ara'aital ladhī yukadhdhibu biddīn.
Fadhālikal ladhī yadu'-'ul yatīm.
Wa lā yaḥuḍḍu 'alā ṭa'āmil miskīn.
Fawailul lil muṣallīn.
Alladhīna hum 'an ṣalātihim sāhūn.
Alladhīna hum yurā'ūn.
Wa yamna'ūnal mā'ūn.

In the name of Allāh, the Most Merciful, the Most Kind.
Have you seen him who denies the religion (the judgement)?
It is he who (harshly) pushes aside the orphan,
and does not urge others to feed the poor and the needy.
Woe to those who do their Ṣalāh
but are forgetful of their Ṣalāh,
who show off
but refuse to give even the smallest help to others.

10 Sūrah Quraish (106) سُورَةُ قُرَيْش

بِسْمِ ٱللَّهِ ٱلرَّحْمَٰنِ ٱلرَّحِيمِ

لِإِيلَٰفِ قُرَيْشٍ . إِۦلَٰفِهِمْ رِحْلَةَ ٱلشِّتَآءِ وَٱلصَّيْفِ . فَلْيَعْبُدُوا۟ رَبَّ
هَٰذَا ٱلْبَيْتِ . ٱلَّذِىٓ أَطْعَمَهُم مِّن جُوعٍ وَءَامَنَهُم مِّنْ خَوْفٍۭ .

Bismillāhir raḥmānir raḥīm.
Li īlāfi quraish.
Īlāfihim riḥlatash shitā'i waṣ-ṣaif.
Falya'budū rabba hādhal bait.
Alladhī aṭ'amahum min jū'in wa āmanahum min khawf.

In the name of Allāh, the Most Merciful, the Most Kind.
For the tradition of the Quraish;
their tradition of travelling in winter and summer.
So they should worship the Lord of this house,
Who has fed them and protected them from hunger, and made them safe from fear.

11 Sūratul Fīl (105) سُورَةُ الْفِيل

بِسْمِ ٱللَّهِ ٱلرَّحْمَٰنِ ٱلرَّحِيمِ

أَلَمْ تَرَ كَيْفَ فَعَلَ رَبُّكَ بِأَصْحَٰبِ ٱلْفِيلِ . أَلَمْ يَجْعَلْ كَيْدَهُمْ
فِي تَضْلِيلٍ . وَأَرْسَلَ عَلَيْهِمْ طَيْرًا أَبَابِيلَ . تَرْمِيهِم بِحِجَارَةٍ
مِّن سِجِّيلٍ . فَجَعَلَهُمْ كَعَصْفٍ مَّأْكُولٍۭ .

Bismillāhir raḥmānir raḥīm.
Alam tara kaifa fa'ala rabbuka bi aṣḥābil fīl.
Alam yaj'al kaidahum fī taḍlīl.
Wa arsala 'alaihim ṭairan abābīl.
Tarmīhim biḥijāratim min sijjīl.
Faja'alahum ka'aṣfim ma'kūl.

In the name of Allāh, the Most Merciful, the Most Kind.
Have you not seen how your Lord dealt with the people of the elephant?
Did He not make their schemes to be nothing,
and send against them flocks of birds,
which pelted them with stones of hard-baked clay?
Thus he made them like eaten straw.

Āyatul Kursī ءَايَةُ ٱلْكُرْسِيِّ 7

Allāh has revealed a verse in the *Qur'ān* called *Āyatul Kursī* (*Sūratul Baqarah* 2:255) which is extra special. Prophet *Muḥammad* ﷺ said, "The greatest verse in the Book of Allāh is: *'Allāh! There is no god but Him, the Ever-living, the One Who Sustains and Protects all that exists.'*" *(Muslim)*

He ﷺ also said, "When you go to your bed, recite *Āyatul Kursī*: *'Allāh! There is no god but Him, the Ever-living, the One Who Sustains and Protects all that exists,'* to the end, for then there will remain over you a guardian from Allāh, and *Shaiṭān* will not come near you until morning." *(al-Bukhārī)*

ٱللَّهُ لَآ إِلَٰهَ إِلَّا هُوَ ٱلْحَيُّ ٱلْقَيُّومُ
لَا تَأْخُذُهُۥ سِنَةٌ وَلَا نَوْمٌ
لَّهُۥ مَا فِي ٱلسَّمَٰوَٰتِ وَمَا فِي ٱلْأَرْضِ
مَن ذَا ٱلَّذِي يَشْفَعُ عِندَهُۥٓ إِلَّا بِإِذْنِهِۦ
يَعْلَمُ مَا بَيْنَ أَيْدِيهِمْ وَمَا خَلْفَهُمْ
وَلَا يُحِيطُونَ بِشَيْءٍ مِّنْ عِلْمِهِۦٓ إِلَّا بِمَا شَآءَ
وَسِعَ كُرْسِيُّهُ ٱلسَّمَٰوَٰتِ وَٱلْأَرْضَ
وَلَا يَـُٔودُهُۥ حِفْظُهُمَا
وَهُوَ ٱلْعَلِيُّ ٱلْعَظِيمُ.

Allāhu lā ilāha illa huwal ḥaiyul qaiyūm,	Allāh! There is no god but Him, the Ever-living, the One Who Sustains and Protects all that exists.
Lā ta'khudhuhū sinatuw wa lā nawm,	Neither slumber nor sleep overtake Him.

Lahū mā fis samāwāti wa mā fil arḍ,	To Him belongs whatever is in the heavens and on the earth.
Man dhal ladhī yashfa'u 'indahū illā bi'idhnih,	Who is he that can intercede with Him except with His permission?
Ya'lamu mā baina aidīhim wa mā khalfahum,	He knows what happens to them (His creatures) in this world, and what will happen to them in the Hereafter.
Wa lā yuḥīṭūna bishai'im min 'ilmihī illā bimā shā',	And they will never compass anything of His knowledge except that which He wills.
Wa si'a kursiyyuhus samāwāti wal arḍ	His *Kursī* extends over the heavens and the earth,
Wa lā ya'ūduhū ḥifẓuhuma,	And He feels no fatigue in guarding and preserving them.
Wa huwal 'aliyyul 'aẓīm.	And He is the Most High, the Most Great.

Adapted from *The Meaning of the Noble Qur'ān*, an English translation of the *Qur'ān* by Dr Muḥammad Taqī-ud-Dīn Al-Hilālī and Dr Muḥammad Muḥsin Khān.

Luqmān's advice to his son 8

Luqmān was a good person, mentioned by Allāh in these verses from the *Qur'ān:*

And (remember) when *Luqmān* said to his son when he was advising him: *"O my son! Do not join others in worship with Allāh. Indeed, joining others in worship with Allāh is the highest wrong-doing."*

And We have enjoined on man (to be dutiful and good) to his parents. His mother bore him in weakness and hardship upon weakness and hardship, and his weaning is two years—give thanks to Me and to your parents—unto Me is the final destination.

But if they (both) strive with you to make you join in worship with Me others that of which you have no knowledge, then obey them not, but behave with them in the world kindly, and follow the path of him who turns to Me in repentance and in obedience. Then to Me will be your return, and I shall tell you what you used to do.

"O my son! If it be (anything) equal to the weight of a grain of mustard seed, and though it be (hidden) in a rock, or in the heavens or in the earth, Allāh will bring it forth. Indeed, Allāh is Subtle (in bringing out that grain), Well-Aware (of its place).

"O my son! Establish Ṣalāh, enjoin Ma'rūf (right) and forbid Munkar (wrong), and bear with patience whatever befalls you. Indeed, these are some of the important commandments ordered by Allāh with no exemption.

"And turn not your face away from men with pride, nor walk (arrogantly) through the earth. Indeed, Allāh likes not each arrogant boaster.

"And be moderate (or show no insolence) in your walking, and lower your voice. Indeed, the harshest of all voices is the voice (braying) of the ass."

(*Sūrah Luqmān* 31:13-19)

Adapted from *The Meaning of the Noble Qur'ān*, an English translation of the *Qur'ān* by Dr Muḥammad Taqī-ud-Dīn Al-Hilālī and Dr Muḥammad Muḥsin Khān.

Selected Qur'ānic verses on Ma'rūf and Munkar

9

بَعْضُ ٱلْأَيَاتِ ٱلْمُخْتَارَةِ مِنَ ٱلْقُرْآنِ ٱلْكَرِيمِ فِي ٱلْأَمْرِ بِٱلْمَعْرُوفِ وَٱلنَّهْيِ عَنِ ٱلْمُنْكَرِ

Ma'rūf ٱلْمَعْرُوف

1 وَأْمُرْ بِٱلْمَعْرُوفِ *Wa'mur bil ma'rūf*
"And promote what is good" (*Sūrah Luqmān* 31:17)

2 وَأَقِيمُوا۟ ٱلصَّلَوٰةَ *Wa aqīmuṣ Ṣalāh*
"And establish Ṣalāh" (*Sūratul Baqarah* 2:83)

3 ٱدْعُ إِلَىٰ سَبِيلِ رَبِّكَ بِٱلْحِكْمَةِ وَٱلْمَوْعِظَةِ ٱلْحَسَنَةِ
Ud'u ilā sabīli rabbika bil ḥikmati wal maw'iẓatil ḥasanah
"Call to the way of your Lord with wisdom and beautiful expressions" (*Sūratun Naḥl* 16:125)

4 وَكُلُوا۟ مِمَّا رَزَقَكُمُ ٱللَّهُ حَلَٰلًا طَيِّبًا
Wa kulū mimmā razaqakumullāhu ḥalālan ṭaiyibā
"And eat of that which Allāh has bestowed on you as food lawful and good" (*Sūratul Mā'idah* 5:88)

5 وَٱعْتَصِمُوا۟ بِحَبْلِ ٱللَّهِ جَمِيعًا *Wa'taṣimū biḥablillāhi jamī'ā*
"And hold fast, all of you together, to the rope of Allāh" (*Sūrah Āli 'Imrān* 3:103)

6 وَتَعَاوَنُوا۟ عَلَى ٱلْبِرِّ وَٱلتَّقْوَىٰ *Wa ta'āwanū 'alal birri wat taqwā*
"And help one another in righteousness and pious duty" (*Sūratul Mā'idah* 5:2)

7 وَأَطِيعُوا۟ ٱللَّهَ وَرَسُولَهُۥ *Wa aṭī'ullāha wa rasūlah*
"And obey Allāh and His messenger" (*Sūratul Anfāl* 8:1)

8 وَتَوَاصَوْا۟ بِٱلْحَقِّ وَتَوَاصَوْا۟ بِٱلصَّبْرِ
Wa tawāṣaw bil ḥaqqi wa tawāṣaw biṣ ṣabr
"And encourage one another to truth and exhort one another to be steadfast" (*Sūratul 'Aṣr* 103:3)

9 وَبِٱلْوَٰلِدَيْنِ إِحْسَـٰنًا *Wa bil wālidaini iḥsānā*
"And be kind to your parents" (*Sūratul Isrā'* 17:23)

10 وَقُولُوا۟ لِلنَّاسِ حُسْنًا *Wa qūlū linnāsi ḥusnā*
"And speak kindly to people" (*Sūratul Baqarah* 2:83)

11 وَأَوْفُوا۟ بِٱلْعَهْدِ *Wa awfū bil 'ahd*
"And keep your covenant" (*Sūratul Isrā'* 17:34)

12 وَلَذِكْرُ ٱللَّهِ أَكْبَرُ *Wa ladhikrullāhi akbar*
"And rememberance of Allāh is the greatest thing"
(*Sūratul 'Ankabūt* 29:45)

13 قَدْ أَفْلَحَ مَن زَكَّىٰهَا *Qad aflaḥa man zakkāhā*
"He is successful who purifies his soul" (*Sūratush Shams* 91:9)

14 ٱدْخُلُوا۟ فِى ٱلسِّلْمِ كَآفَّةً *Udkhulū fissilmi kāffah*
"Enter into Islām completely" (*Sūratul Baqarah* 2:208)

15 حَـٰفِظُوا۟ عَلَى ٱلصَّلَوَٰتِ *Ḥāfiẓū 'alaṣ ṣalawāt*
"Guard your Ṣalāh" (*Sūratul Baqarah* 2:238)

16 وَٱشْكُرُوا۟ لِلَّهِ *Washkurū lillāh*
"And be thankful to Allah" (*Sūratul Baqarah* 2:172)

17 وَاسْتَعِينُوا۟ بِٱلصَّبْرِ وَٱلصَّلَوٰةِ *Wasta'īnū biṣ ṣabri waṣ ṣalāh*
"And seek help with patience and Ṣalāh" (*Sūratul Baqarah* 2:45)

18 وَاسْتَغْفِرْ لِذَنۢبِكَ *Wastaghfir lidhambik*
"And ask forgiveness for your sins" (*Sūrah Muḥammad* 47:19)

19 وَتُوبُوٓا۟ إِلَى ٱللَّهِ جَمِيعًا *Wa tūbū ilallāhi jamī'a*
"And turn unto Allāh together" (*Sūratun Nūr* 24:31)

20 وَرَتِّلِ ٱلْقُرْءَانَ تَرْتِيلًا *Wa rattilil qur'āna tartīlā*
"And recite the Qur'ān calmly and distinctly (with attention to its meaning)" (*Sūratul Muzzammil* 73:4)

21 وَأَنفِقُوا۟ فِى سَبِيلِ ٱللَّهِ *Wa anfiqū fī sabīlillāh*
"And spend your wealth in the way of Allāh" (*Sūratul Baqarah* 2:195)

Munkar ٱلْمُنكَر

1 وَٱنْهَ عَنِ ٱلْمُنكَرِ *Wanha 'anil munkar*
"And forbid what is wrong" (*Sūrah Luqmān* 31:17)

2 وَلَا تَلْبِسُوا۟ ٱلْحَقَّ بِٱلْبَٰطِلِ *Wa lā talbisul ḥaqqa bil bāṭil*
"And do not muddle truth with falsehood" (*Sūratul Baqarah* 2:42)

3 لَا تُشْرِكْ بِٱللَّهِ *Lā tushrik billāh*
"Do not make partners with Allāh" (*Sūrah Luqmān* 31:13)

4 وَٱجْتَنِبُوا۟ قَوْلَ ٱلزُّورِ *Wajtanibū qawlaz zūr*
"And give up telling lies" (*Sūratul Ḥajj* 22:30)

5 وَلَا يَغْتَب بَّعْضُكُم بَعْضًا *Wa lā yaghtab ba'ḍukum ba'ḍā*
"And do not backbite one another" (*Sūratul Ḥujurāt* 49:12)

6 وَلَا تَجَسَّسُوا۟ *Wa lā tajassasū*
"And do not spy on each other" (*Sūratul Ḥujurāt* 49:12)

7 وَلَا تَلْمِزُوٓا۟ أَنفُسَكُمْ *Wa lā talmizū anfusakum*
"And do not insult one another" (*Sūratul Ḥujurāt* 49:11)

8 وَلَا تَقْرَبُوا۟ ٱلزِّنَىٰٓ *Wa lā taqrabuz zinā*
"And do not come near adultery" (*Sūratul Isrā'* 17:32)

9 وَلَا يُبْدِينَ زِينَتَهُنَّ إِلَّا لِبُعُولَتِهِنَّ...
Wa lā yubdīna zīnatahunna illā libu'ūlatahinna...
"And (tell the believing women) not to reveal their beauty except to their husbands..." (*Sūratun Nūr* 24:31)

10 وَلَا تَكْتُمُوا۟ ٱلشَّهَـٰدَةَ *Wa lā taktumush shahādah*
"And do not hide your testimony" (*Sūratul Baqarah* 2:283)

11 وَلَا تَمْشِ فِى ٱلْأَرْضِ مَرَحًا *Wa lā tamshi fil arḍi maraḥā*
"And do not walk on the earth arrogantly" (*Sūratul Isrā'* 17:37)

12 وَلَا تَنَابَزُوا۟ بِٱلْأَلْقَـٰبِ *Wa lā tanābazū bil alqāb*
"And do not insult one another by nicknames" (*Sūratul Ḥujurāt* 49:11)

13 وَلَا تَقْتُلُوٓا۟ أَوْلَـٰدَكُمْ خَشْيَةَ إِمْلَـٰقٍ
Wa lā taqtulū awlādakum khashyata imlāq
"And do not kill your children in fear of poverty" (*Sūratul Isrā'* 17:31)

14 وَلَا تُبَذِّرْ تَبْذِيرًا *Wa lā tubadhdhir tabdhīrā*
"And do not spend your wealth extravagantly" (*Sūratul Isrā'* 17:26)

15 لِمَ تَقُولُونَ مَا لَا تَفْعَلُونَ *Lima taqūlūna mā lā taf'alūn*
"Why do you say that which you do not do?" (*Sūratuṣ Ṣaff* 61:2)

16 وَحَرَّمَ ٱلرِّبَوٰا *Wa ḥarramar ribā*
"And interest has been prohibited" (*Sūratul Baqarah* 2:275)

17 وَلَا تَقْرَبُوا۟ مَالَ ٱلْيَتِيمِ *Wa lā taqrabū mālal yatīm*
"And come not near to the orphan's property" (*Sūratul An'ām* 6:152)

18 وَلَا تَعَاوَنُوا۟ عَلَى ٱلْإِثْمِ وَٱلْعُدْوَٰنِ *Wa lā ta'āwanū 'alal ithmi wal 'udwān*
"And do not help one another in sin and enmity" (*Sūratul Mā'idah* 5:2)

Declaration of Faith اَلشَّهَادَة 10

1 Al-Kalimatuṭ Ṭaiyibah اَلْكَلِمَةُ الطَّيِّبَة

لَآ إِلٰهَ إِلَّا اللّٰهُ مُحَمَّدٌ رَسُوْلُ اللّٰهِ

Lā ilāha illallāhu Muḥammadur rasūlullāh.
There is no god but Allāh; Muḥammad is the messenger of Allāh.

2 Kalimatush Shahādah كَلِمَةُ الشَّهَادَة

أَشْهَدُ اَنْ لَّآ إِلٰهَ إِلَّا اللّٰهُ وَحْدَهُ لَا شَرِيكَ لَهُ
وَأَشْهَدُ اَنَّ مُحَمَّدًا عَبْدُهُ وَرَسُولُهُ

Ash-hadu allā ilāha illallāhu waḥdahu lā sharīka lahu
wa ash-hadu anna Muḥammadan 'abduhu wa rasūluh.
I testify that there is no god but Allāh and He is One and has no partner
and I testify that Muḥammad is His servant and messenger.

3 Al-Īmānul Mujmal اَلْإِيمَانُ الْمُجْمَل

آمَنْتُ بِاللّٰهِ كَمَا هُوَ بِأَسْمَآئِهِ وَصِفَاتِهِ وَقَبِلْتُ جَمِيعَ أَحْكَامِهِ

Āmantu billāhi kamā huwa bi'asmā'ihī wa ṣifātihī wa qabiltu jamī'a aḥkāmih.
I believe in Allāh (as He is) with all His names and attributes
and I accept all His commands.

4 Al-Īmanul Mufaṣṣal

اَلْإِيمَانُ الْمُفَصَّل

آمَنْتُ بِاللّٰهِ وَمَلآئِكَتِهٖ وَكُتُبِهٖ وَرُسُلِهٖ وَالْيَوْمِ الْآخِرِ وَالْقَدْرِ خَيْرِهٖ وَشَرِّهٖ مِنَ اللّٰهِ تَعَالىٰ وَالْبَعْثِ بَعْدَ الْمَوْتِ

Āmantu billāhi, wa malā'ikatihī, wa kutubihī, wa rusulihī, wal yawmil ākhiri, wal qadri khairihī wa sharrihī minallāhi ta'ālā, wal ba'thi ba'dal mawt.

I believe in Allāh, in His angels, in His books, in His messengers, in the last day and in the fact that everything good or bad is decided by Allāh, the Almighty, and in the life after death.

5 Kalimah Raddil Kufr

كَلِمَةُ رَدِّ الْكُفْر

اَللّٰهُمَّ إِنِّي أَعُوذُ بِكَ مِنْ اَنْ أُشْرِكَ بِكَ شَيْئًا وَّأَنَا أَعْلَمُ وَاسْتَغْفِرُكَ لِمَا لَآ أَعْلَمُ إِنَّكَ أَنْتَ عَلَّامُ الْغُيُوبِ تُبْتُ عَنْهُ وَتَبَرَّأْتُ عَنْ كُلِّ دِينٍ سِوٰى دِينِ الْإِسْلَامِ وَأَسْلَمْتُ وَأَقُولُ لَآ إِلٰهَ إِلَّا اللّٰهُ مُحَمَّدٌ رَسُولُ اللّٰهِ

Allāhumma innī a'ūdhu bika min an ushrika bika shai'aw wa ana a'lamu wastaghfiruka limā lā a'lamu innaka anta 'allāmul ghuyūbi tubtu 'anhu wa tabarra'tu 'an kulli dīnin siwā dīnil islāmi wa aslamtu wa aqūlu lā ilāha illallāhu muḥammadur rasūlullāh.

O Allāh, surely I do seek refuge in You from making any partner with You knowingly; I beg Your forgiveness for the sins which I am not aware of; surely, You are the knower of all secrets. I repent for all the sins and make myself proof against all religions except Islām and I accepted it and declare that there is no god but Allāh, Muḥammad is the messenger of Allāh.

Glossary of Islāmic Words and Terms

It is difficult to translate Arabic terms into English (or any other language), especially those used in the Qur'ān and the *Aḥādīth*. A brief explanation of the meaning of the important Arabic words used in this book is given below:

ﷺ	صَلَّى اللهُ عَلَيْهِ وَسَلَّم	The Arabic *Ṣallallāhu 'alaihi wasallam*, written after the name of Prophet *Muḥammad* ﷺ, meaning 'peace and blessings of Allāh be upon him.
Adhān	أَذَان	The call to *Ṣalāh*.
Aḥādīth	أَحَادِيث	(sing. *Ḥadīth*) Reports of the sayings, deeds and actions approved by Prophet *Muḥammad* ﷺ.
Ākhirah	آخِرَة	Life after death. It includes the Day of Judgement and the never-ending life after death.
Allāh	اَللّٰه	The proper name of God. Allāh is the Maker of all creatures. He is not just the God of Muslims, but of all human kind.
Āmīn	آمِين	The word said after the recitation of *Sūratul Fātiḥah* or any *du'ā'* to Allāh. The word means: 'Accept our prayer, O Allāh'.
'Arafāt	عَرَفَات	The plain 25km south-east of Makkah where people gather during *Ḥajj*. (2:198)
Arkānul Islām	أَرْكَانُ الْإِسْلَام	The five pillars (or basic duties) of Islām.
'Aṣr	عَصْر	Name of the *Ṣalāh* after mid-afternoon.
Āyah	آيَة	(pl. *Āyāt*) A verse of the *Qur'ān*.
Basmalah	بَسْمَلَة	(see *Tasmiyah*)
Darūd	دَرُود	Reciting *aṣ-Ṣalāh 'alan Nabiyy* during *Ṣalāh* or at any other time. This is a Persian word.
Dhikr	ذِكْر	Remembering or praising Allāh.
Du'ā'	دُعَاء	A supplication to Allāh, or asking Allāh for favour, blessing and mercy.
Fajr	فَجْر	Name of the *Ṣalāh* at dawn.
Farḍ	فَرْض	Compulsory duty prescribed by Allāh.
Farḍu Kifāyah	فَرْضُ كِفَايَة	A collective obligation or duty of the Muslims. When some of the Muslims in an area do this, the obligation is discharged. If no one does it, everyone in the area would be considered sinful — e.g. *Ṣalātul Janāzah*.
Fiqh	فِقْه	Literally 'understanding'. The term refers to the science of Islāmic law or jurisprudence.

Ghair Mu'akkadah (Sunnah)	غَيْر مُؤَكَّدَة	Refers to the *Ṣalāh* performed only occasionally by Prophet *Muḥammad* ﷺ. As opposed to these, there are *Sunnah Mu'akkadah Ṣalāh* which Prophet *Muḥammad* ﷺ performed regularly, e.g. 2 *rak'ahs* of *Sunnah* before *Ṣalātul Fajr*.
al-Ghurrul Muḥajjalūn	اَلغُرُّ المُحَجَّلُون	Meaning 'distinctly bright'. The parts of the body of the Muslims washed during *Wuḍū'* will shine on the Day of Resurrection and angels will call them by this name.
Ghusl	غُسْل	Washing the whole body for *Ṭahārah*. (4:43; 5:6)
Ḥadīth	حَدِيث	(pl. *Aḥādīth*) A report of a saying, deed or action approved by Prophet *Muḥammad* ﷺ.
Ḥalāl	حَلاَل	That which is lawful (permitted) in Islām.
Ḥarām	حَرَام	That which is unlawful (forbidden) in Islām.
Ḥayā'	حَيَاء	Meaning 'modesty', 'self-respect', 'bashfulness', etc. Refers to the feeling of shame when a bad act is done or something indecent happens.
Hidāyah	هِدَايَة	Guidance from Allāh.
Ḥijāb	حِجَاب	A Muslim woman's veil or head-covering when meeting strangers and going out.
'Ibādah	عِبَادَة	Translated as 'worship', it refers to any permitted activity performed to gain Allāh's pleasure.
'Īd	عِيد	A day of celebration: *'Īd ul Fiṭr* comes after the end of *Ramaḍān*, and *'Īd ul Aḍḥā* during *Ḥajj* in the Islāmic month of *Dhū al-Ḥijjah*.
Imām	إِمَام	The person who leads prayer in a congregation, or a leader.
Īmān	إِيمَان	Faith or belief.
al-Īmānul Mufaṣṣal	اَلإِيمَانُ الْمُفَصَّل	The faith in detail.
Iqāmah	إِقَامَة	The second call to prayer, made when *Ṣalāh* is about to begin in congregation.
'Ishā'	عِشَاء	Name of the *Ṣalāh* at night
Islām	اَلإِسْلاَم	This is the name given by Allāh to the religion for mankind. The word means submission and obedience to Allāh's commands to attain peace in this life and in the *Ākhirah*. It began with the first prophet *Ādam* and was completed at the time of Prophet *Muḥammad* ﷺ.
Istikhārah	إِسْتِخَارَة	(see *Ṣalātul Istikhārah*)
I'tidāl	إِعْتِدَال	Returning to the position of *qiyām* after *rukū'*.
Jahannam	جَهَنَّم	Hell, the place of eternal suffering.

Jamā‘ah جَمَاعَة Congregation, when people say *Ṣalāh* as one group.

Janāzah جَنَازَة The funeral *Ṣalāh*.

Jannah جَنَّة Heaven, the place of eternal bliss. Literally ‘Garden’, also called Paradise.

Jibrā’īl جِبْرَائِيل The angel (Gabriel) who brought revelation from Allāh. (2:97–98).

Jihād جِهَاد One of the important duties in Islām, it means to strive. *Jihād fī sabī lillāh* (Striving for the sake of Allāh) means exerting all our efforts to establish *Ma‘rūf* and remove *Munkar* from society in order to gain Allāh’s pleasure.

Jinn جِنّ Allāh’s creatures with free will, created from smokeless fire.

Jumu‘ah (see *Ṣalātul Jumu‘ah*)

Ka‘bah كَعْبَة The first place built for the worship of Allāh, in Makkah. Also called ‘The House of Allāh’ *(Baitullāh)*.

Kāfir كَافِر (pl. *Kāfirūn* or *Kuffār*) A person who does not believe in Islām.

al-Kalimatuṭ Ṭaiyibah اَلْكَلِمَةُ الطَّيِّبَة The pure sentence, i.e. the words said in *ash-Shahādah*.

Khalīfah خَلِيفَة An agent or vicegerent of Allāh on earth.

Khuṭbah خُطْبَة The sermon given before *Ṣalātul Jumu‘ah*. Usually a lecture about Islām.

Maghrib مَغْرِب Name of the *Ṣalāh* just after sunset.

Makkah مَكَّة The city where the *Ka‘bah* is located and the birth place of Prophet *Muḥammad* ﷺ. Also called Bakkah in the *Qur’ān*. (3:96)

Makrūh مَكْرُوه Those things which are disliked and are reprehensible in Islāmic *Sharī‘ah*.

Masjid مَسْجِد Literally ‘a place of prostration’. A mosque.

Mu’adhdhin مُؤَذِّن The person who calls the *Adhān*.

Muḥammad ﷺ مُحَمَّد ﷺ The final messenger of Allāh to mankind. He was Muḥammad bin ‘Abdullāh.

Munkar مُنْكَر Wrong actions. Its opposite is *Ma‘rūf* (right).

Muqīm مُقِيم A local resident.

Muqtadī مُقْتَدِي A Muslim who prays behind an *Imām*.

Musāfir مُسَافِر A traveller.

Muṣallī مُصَلِّي A person saying *Ṣalāh*.

Muslim مُسْلِم A person who freely and consciously accepts the Islāmic way of life, and sincerely practices it.

Nafl	نَفل	Optional.
Naẓāfah	نَظَافَة	Cleanliness.
Niyyah	نِيَّة	Intention.
Qaḍā'	قَضَاء	Making up for a missed prayer.
Qiblah	قِبلَة	The direction towards the *Ka'bah* in *Makkah* to which Muslims face during *Ṣalāh*.
Qirā'ah	قِرَاءَة	Reciting the *Qur'ān* during *Ṣalāh*.
Qiyām	قِيَام	Standing upright in *Ṣalāh*.
Qunūt	اَلْقُنُوت	The special *du'ā'* said during *Ṣalātul Witr.*
Qur'ān	اَلْقُرآن	The sacred book of Muslims, the final book of guidance from Allāh, sent down to *Muḥammad* ﷺ through the angel *Jibrā'īl* (Gabriel) over a period of 23 years.
Qu'ūd	اَلْقُعود	Sitting after prostration in *Ṣalāh*.
Rak'ah	رَكْعَة	(pl. *Raka'āt*) A 'unit' of *Ṣalāh*, each *Ṣalāh* having two, three or four *rak'ahs*.
Ramaḍān	رَمَضَان	Ninth month of the Islāmic calendar, the month of obligatory fasting.
Rukū'	رُكُوع	Bowing during *Ṣalāh*.
Sajdatus Sahw	سَجْدَةُ السَّهو	Prostrations to make up for a mistake made during *Ṣalāh*.
Ṣalāh	صَلَاة	The compulsory prayer, offered at fives set times every day in a particular way.
Salām	سَلَام	Turning the head to the right and left at the end of *Ṣalāh*, saying *Assalāmu 'alaikum wa raḥmatullāh*.
aṣ-Ṣalātu 'alan Nabiyy	اَلصَّلَاةُ عَلَى النَّبِي	The *Darūd* recited after *at-Tashahhud* at the end of a particular *Ṣalāh*.
Ṣalātul Istikhārah	صَلَاةُ الْإِسْتِخَارَة	A prayer for seeking Allāh's guidance on a matter.
Ṣalātul Jumu'ah	صَلَاةُ الْجُمُعَة	The special congregational *Ṣalāh* said at midday every Friday.
Ṣawm	صَوم	Fasting in the month of *Ramaḍān*, one of the five pillars (basic duties) of Islām.
Shahādah	شَهَادَة	Testifying that "There is no god but Allāh, *Muḥammad* is Allāh's messenger". The first pillar (basic duty) of Islām.
Sujūd	سُجُوْد	Prostrating during *Ṣalāh*.
Sunnah	سُنَّة	(pl. *Sunan*) The example of Prophet *Muḥammad* ﷺ in what he did, said and approved. Also, the additional *Ṣalāh* practised by Prophet *Muḥammad* ﷺ.

Sūrah	سُورَة	(pl. *Suwar*) A chapter of the *Qur'ān*.
Ta'awwudh	تَعَوُّذ	Saying *A'ūdhu billāhi minash shaiṭānir rajīm*.
Tahajjud	تَهَجُّد	Optional *Ṣalāh* between midnight and dawn.
Ṭahārah	طَهَارَة	To be clean and pure.
Takbīr	تَكْبِير	Saying *Allāhu Akbar.*
Takbīratul Iḥrām	تَكْبِيْرَةُ الإِحْرَام	Saying *Allāhu Akbar* at the start of the *Ṣalāh*.
Tarāwīḥ	تَرَاوِيح	The special *Ṣalāh* said after *'Ishā'* in *Ramaḍān*.
Tasbiḥ	تَسْبِيح	Saying *Subḥāna rabbiyal…* (Glorification of Allāh).
Tashahhud	تَشَهُّد	The recitation after two *rak'ahs* and at the end of *Ṣalāh*.
Tasmiyah	تَسْمِيَة	Saying *Bismillāhir raḥmānir raḥīm.* Also called the *Basmalah*.
Tayammum	تَيَمُّم	Dry ablution, performed when water is scarce, unavailable or when using it would be harmful.
Thanā'	ثَنَاء	Meaning 'praise' or 'appreciation'. Saying *Subḥānaka allāhumma…* after *Takbīratul Iḥrām*.
Wājib	وَاجِب	Obligatory.
Witr	وِتْر	Literally 'odd' (opposite of even). Refers to the *Ṣalāh* offered after *'Ishā'*.
Wuḍū'	وُضُوْء	Washing for *Ṣalāh* in a prescribed way.
Zakāh	زَكَاة	Welfare contribution — a compulsory payment from a Muslim's annual savings, one of the five pillars (basic duties) of Islām. It is an act of *'Ibādah* (worship) and should not be confused with any tax.
Ẓuhr	ظُهْر	Name of the *Ṣalāh* just after midday.